WOME
OF TH
WORD

BIBLE
STUDY
SERIES

CAPTIVATED BY GOD

EADIE GOODBOY
AND AGNES C. LAWLESS

Gospel Light

Published by Gospel Light
Ventura, California, U.S.A.
www.gospellight.com
Printed in the U.S.A.

Aglow International is an interdenominational organization of
Christian women. Our mission is to lead women to Jesus Christ and provide
opportunity for Christian women to grow in their faith and minister to others.
Our publications are used to help women find a personal relationship with
Jesus Christ, to enhance growth in their Christian experience, and to help them
recognize their roles and relationships according to Scripture. For more
information about our organization, please write to Aglow International,
P.O. Box 1749, Edmonds, WA 98020-1749, U.S.A., or call (425) 775-7282.
For ordering or information about the Aglow studies and other
resources, visit the Aglow E-store at www.aglow.org.

Rights for publishing this book outside the U.S.A. or in non-English languages are
administered by Gospel Light Worldwide, an international not-for-profit ministry.
For additional information, please visit www.glww.org, email info@glww.org, or write
to Gospel Light Worldwide, 1957 Eastman Avenue, Ventura, CA 93003, U.S.A.

To order copies of this book and other Gospel Light products in bulk quantities,
please contact us at 1-800-446-7735.

ONTENTS

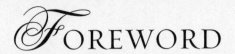OREWORD

When the apostle Paul poured out his heart in letters to the young churches in Asia, he was responding to his apostolic call to shepherd those tender flocks. They needed encouragement in their new life in Jesus. They needed solid doctrine. They needed truth from someone who had an intimate relationship with God and with them.

Did Paul know as he was writing that these simple letters would form the bulk of the New Testament? We can be confident that the Holy Spirit did! How like God to use Paul's relationship with these churches to cement His plan and purpose in their lives, and, generations later, in ours.

We in Aglow can relate to Paul's desire to bond those young churches together in the faith. After 1967, when Aglow fellowships began bubbling up across the United States and in other countries, they needed encouragement. They needed to know the fullness of who they were in Christ. They needed relationship. Like Paul, our desire to reach out and nurture from far away birthed a series of Bible studies that have fed thousands since 1973 when our first study, *Genesis*, was published. Our studies share heart to heart, giving Christians new insights about themselves and their relationship with and in God.

In 1998, God's generous nature provided us a rewarding new relationship with Gospel Light. Together we published our Aglow classics as well as a selection of exciting new studies. Gospel Light began as a publishing ministry much in the same way Aglow began publishing Bible studies. Henrietta Mears formed Gospel Light in response to requests from churches across America for the Sunday School materials she had written. Gospel Light remains a strong ministry-minded witness for the gospel around the world.

Our heart's desire is that these studies will continue to kindle the minds of women and men, touch their hearts, and refresh their spirits with the light and life a loving Savior abundantly supplies.

This study, *Captivated by God* by Eadie Goodboy and Agnes Lawless, will guide you in your quest to know your heavenly Father better and to mold your character to be more like His. I know its contents will reward you richly.

Jane Hansen Hoyt
International President
Aglow International

INTRODUCTION

The new baby is presented to her relatives at a dinner party. Family members peer at her. Her features and expressions are scrutinized.

"Look at that darling nose!" declares her grandmother. "She definitely inherited it from our side of the family."

"Did you see her smile?" says an aunt. "She looks just like her dad."

As the baby grows, she becomes more and more like her father. Her appearance, mannerisms, expressions and behavior show that she is truly her father's daughter.

This is true not only in the physical realm but in the spiritual as well. Like any parent, our heavenly Father wants His children to resemble Him and, while He was on earth, Jesus was "the radiance of God's glory and the exact representation of his being" (Hebrews 1:3) and "the image of the invisible God, the firstborn over all creation" (Colossians 1:15).

As the adopted children of God, "we are heirs—heirs of God and co-heirs with Christ" (Romans 8:17), and we "are being transformed into his likeness with ever-increasing glory" (2 Corinthians 3:18).

To grow increasingly like our Father, it is essential that we know what He is like. As we study the attributes, or the character, of God, we will learn to know Him better and become more and more like Him.

AN OVERVIEW OF THE STUDY

This Bible study is divided into four sections:

1. *A Closer Look at the Problem* defines the problem and the goal of the lesson.

2. *A Closer Look at God's Truth* gets you into God's Word. What does God have to say about the problem? How can you begin to apply God's Word as you work through each lesson?

3. *A Closer Look at My Own Heart* will help you clarify and further apply Bible truth in your own life. It will also give guidance as you work toward change.

4. *Action Steps I Can Take Today* is designed to help you concentrate on immediate steps of action.

WHAT YOU WILL NEED

· *A Bible*—The main Bible used in this study is the *New International Version,* but you can use whatever Bible translation you are used to reading.

· *A Notebook*—During this study you will want to keep a journal to record what God shows you personally. You may also want to journal additional thoughts or feelings that come up as you go through the lessons. Some questions may require more space than is given in this study book.

· *Time to Meditate*—Only through meditation on what you're learning will you hear God's Word for you and begin to experience a heart knowledge, as well as a head knowledge, of the subject of being captivated by God. Give the Holy Spirit time to personalize His Word to your heart so that you can know what your response should be to the knowledge you are gaining.

How to Start and Lead a Small Group

One key to leading a small group is to ask yourself, *What would Jesus do and how would He do it?* Jesus began His earthly ministry with a small group called the disciples, and the fact of His presence made wherever He was a safe place to be. Think of a small group as a safe place. It is a place that reflects God's heart and His hands. The way in which Jesus lived and worked with His disciples is a basic small-group model that we are able to draw both direction and nurture from.

Paul exhorted us to "walk in love, as Christ also has loved us and given Himself for us" (Ephesians 5:2, *NKJV*). We, as His earthly reflections, are privileged to walk in His footsteps, to help bind up the brokenhearted as He did or simply to listen with a compassionate heart. Whether you use this book as a Bible study, or as a focus point for a support group, a church group or a home group, walking in love means that we "bear one another's burdens" (Galatians 6:2, *NKJV*). The loving atmosphere provided by a small group can nourish, sustain and lift us up as nothing else can.

Jesus walked in love and spoke from an honest heart. In His endless well of compassion He never misplaced truth. Rather, He surrounded it with mercy. Those who left His presence felt good about themselves because Jesus used truth to point them in the right direction for their lives. When He spoke about the sinful woman who washed Jesus' feet with her tears and wiped them with her hair, He did not deny her sin. He said, "Her sins, which are many, are forgiven, for she loved much" (Luke 7:47, *NKJV*). That's honesty without condemnation.

Jesus was a model of servant leadership (see Mark 10:43-44). One of the key skills a group leader possesses is the ability to be an encourager of the group's members to grow spiritually. Keeping in personal contact with each member of the group, especially if one is absent, tells each one that he or she is important to the group. Other skills an effective group leader demonstrates include being a good listener, guiding the discussion, as well as guiding the group to deal with any conflicts that arise within it.

Whether you're a veteran or brand new to small-group leadership, virtually every group you lead will be different in personality and dynamic. The constant is the presence of Jesus Christ, and when He is at the group's center, everything else will come together.

*Y*OU'RE INVITED!

TO GROW . . .

To develop and reach maturity; thrive; to spring up;
come into existence from a source;

WITH A GROUP . . .

An assemblage of persons gathered or located together;
a number of individuals considered together because of similarities;

TO EXPLORE . . .

To investigate systematically; examine; search into or range over
for the purpose of discovery;

NEW TOPICS

Subject of discussion or conversation.

*M*EETING

Date _____ Time _____

Place _____

_____

Contact _____

Phone _____

ONE

OUR LIKENESS TO GOD

"You look just like your mother," an old friend exclaims as you slip into a navy-blue blouse that brings out the blue of your eyes.

As the years roll by, you catch yourself acting more and more like her, too. You roll out pie dough and then rub the back of your hands on the thighs of your blue jeans. Your daughter runs to you when she's scraped her knee—you kiss the owie and make it well.

You realize then that it's in the genes—like mother, like daughter. And the process has only just begun.

Which of your parents are you most like? In what ways are you like your mother or your father?

_____
_____
_____
_____
_____

Take one characteristic that you admire about your mother or father and tell how you would like to see it developed in your own life.

_____
_____
_____
_____

A Closer Look at the Problem

When we became Christians, we were born into the spiritual family of God. At our new birth, God planted His Spirit within us. Then comes the process of slowly transforming us into the likeness of His Son, Jesus.

But how can this be? you may wonder. God is vast and wonderful and His characteristics are vast and wonderful, too. He even says in Isaiah 55:8-9 that His thoughts and ways are beyond our understanding.

Yes, great mystery surrounds the nature of God. Yet God *is* knowable. Paul said that because He is, we can be like Him, for we "are being transformed into his likeness with ever-increasing glory" (2 Corinthians 3:18). God literally accomplishes a life-changing transformation for those who truly believe in Jesus Christ.

But how does it happen? Can frail imperfect humans really be like God? If so, how can we be participants with Him in this amazing transformation?

One of the things we can do is study God's characteristics, or attributes, as revealed in His Word—His mercy, faithfulness, love and many other attributes all express who He is and how we should respond to Him.

This chapter will help us gain insight into how we are slowly being transformed into His image. We'll delve into Paul's epistles and then go with Moses to the top of the mountain to be with God. Together we will discover more about how we can be like Jesus.

A Closer Look at God's Truth

Conforming Us to His Image

Perhaps no writer was more aware of the process of being conformed into the image of Christ than was the apostle Paul. Read Romans 8:28-29. What is one of God's great purposes in redeeming us?

_____

_____

_____

_____

_____

Read Philippians 1:6. How long does this process of conforming take?

_____

_____

_____

_____

Read 1 Corinthians 2:12-16 and 6:11. What part does the Holy Spirit have in this process?

_____

_____

_____

_____

_____

Read Romans 8:14-18. What are those who are led by the Spirit called (see verses 14, 16)?

_____

_____

_____

_____

_____

What is the ultimate goal of being led by the Spirit and conformed to Christ's image (see verse 17)?

_____

_____

_____

_____

What must we experience before sharing His glory (see verses 17-18; also Hebrews 5:8)?

_____

_____

_____

_____

Describe the kind of suffering you think is referred to in Romans 8:17-18 and in Philippians 3:10.

_____

_____

_____

_____

What kind of suffering have you experienced? Could any of it be described as "sharing in his sufferings" (Philippians 3:10)?

_____
_____
_____
_____

EQUIPPING US TO REIGN
If you have suffered with Christ, what responsibilities do you think you were (or are) being trained for?

_____
_____
_____
_____

Complete the following verses:

If we _____, we will also _____ with him (2 Timothy 2:12).

You have made them to be a _____ and _____ to _____ our God, and they will _____ on the earth (Revelation 5:10).

Not only will Christ reign as King of kings, but we, too, are designed to reign with Him. Now we can better understand why we experience sufferings and trials.

During our years on earth, the Holy Spirit is maturing and equipping us to rule. If royal heirs to secular kingdoms are placed in schools demanding much study and highly disciplined training, how much more do the children of God need training to be spiritually strong and to wisely rule others?

When trials come into your life, do you feel that you are being punished or that you are being equipped to rule with Jesus? Explain your answer.

_____
_____
_____
_____

If you understood that trials were God's loving way of maturing and training you for His great purposes, would it make a difference in your attitude? How?

_____

_____

_____

_____

_____

Can you see through present or past trials and recognize that all things
are working together for your good (see Romans 8:28)? Share a particular
time of testing that you can say God has worked together for good in your
life. Explain how.

_____

_____

_____

_____

_____

REFLECTING HIS GLORY
Read Romans 12:1-2. What one thing must we do in order to grow in
Christ's likeness?

_____

_____

_____

_____

_____

Do you love and trust God enough to obey these verses in Romans? If not,
what prevents you from doing so?

_____

_____

_____

_____

What would it take for you to wholeheartedly obey Romans 12:1-2?

_____

_____

_____

_____

_____

Read 2 Corinthians 3:18. Who does the actual transforming?

_____

_____

_____

_____

What part do you think believers might have in this process?

_____

_____

_____

_____

Paul took it for granted that true Christians reflect something of God's glory. However, even as we cannot earn our salvation, neither can we do anything on our own to grow into that glory. The Holy Spirit does the work, but we must offer ourselves and be available to Him. One way we can do this is to spend time with God.

Read Exodus 34:1-10,27-35. According to verse 2, what action was Moses to take?

_____

_____

_____

What did God reveal to Moses about Himself (see verses 6-7)?

_____

_____

_____

How did Moses respond (see verse 8)?

_____

_____

_____

_____

_____

How long was Moses alone with God (see verse 28)?

_____

_____

_____

_____

_____

In what way was Moses changed by his time with God (see verse 29)?

_____

_____

_____

_____

_____

How do Moses' actions compare to what we are entreated to do in Romans 12:1-2?

_____

_____

_____

_____

_____

Read 2 Corinthians 3:7-11; then reread Exodus 34:29-35. Compare the glory Moses received with that which we have available in Christ. Why don't we always have His radiance on our faces?

_____

_____

_____

_____

_____

Reread 2 Corinthians 3:18. To what attributes of God's character (mentioned in 3:7-11) is Paul referring in this verse?

_____

_____

_____

_____

_____

What qualities of the Lord's character would you like to see reflected in your life?

_____

_____

_____

_____

_____

A Closer Look at My Own Heart

ALONE BY YOURSELF

Prayerfully read through the following personal questions that will help you evaluate your relationship with Jesus.

Do I know that I belong to God? If not, will I receive Him now as my Savior and Lord?

_____

_____

_____

_____

Am I comfortable in God's presence? Do I converse freely with Him in prayer?

_____

_____

_____

_____

Is my relationship with the Father one of close, trusting intimacy or does He seem vague and far off? If the latter, what can I do to improve my relationship with Him?

_____

_____

_____

_____

_____

Do I look forward to spending time with the Lord? Is time spent in prayer and Bible reading a pleasure to me?

_____

_____

_____

_____

_____

How much time do I actually spend with God alone each day? How much time do I devote to worship? To prayer? To Bible reading and meditating on His Word?

_____

_____

_____

_____

_____

ALONE WITH GOD

You may not be able to spend 40 days and nights alone with God the way Moses did, but you can take time to be with God. Even Jesus spent time alone with His heavenly Father when He was here on earth.

Read Mark 1:35; 6:46; Luke 5:16; 6:12; 11:1. Why was it important for Jesus to spend time alone with His heavenly Father?

_____

_____

_____

_____

How will time spent alone with the Lord shape you into the image of Christ?

_____

_____

_____

_____

_____

_____

Action Steps I Can Take Today

Prayerful time alone with God in His Word is a living encounter with Jesus Christ Himself—a time when you meet Him face to face. Without spending time in His presence, you cannot grow in likeness to Him.

Will you make a commitment to listen and talk to Him this week? If your answer is yes, you are encouraged to ask a friend to keep you accountable. Check in with your friend several times this week.

Write Psalm 17:15 on an index card and put it beside your bed. Make the verse a part of your evening prayer as you end each day this week with Him.

TWO

THE MERCY
AND FAITHFULNESS
OF GOD

PART ONE: THE MERCY OF GOD

What is mercy? Basically, "mercy" means kindness. "Mercy" is translated from a Hebrew word that has also been translated as "love," "lovingkind-ness" and "compassion." Alexander Pope expressed this mercy in a stanza of his poem "The Universal Prayer":

Teach me to feel another's woe,
To hide the fault I see;
That mercy I to others show
That mercy show to me.[1]

Reread the above stanza. As you do, substitute kindness or one of the words commonly translated as "mercy" for the word "mercy."

A Closer Look at the Problem

In spite of our sins and failures, God's mercy is boundless and ours for the asking. However, we must meet certain conditions before we receive His mercy. We also have a responsibility to pass His mercy on to others. The goal of this second lesson in *Captivated by God* is to help us develop a deepened comprehension of God's mercy and of ourselves as channels of that mercy.

A Closer Look at God's Truth

THE GREATNESS OF GOD'S MERCY

Read 2 Samuel 24:14. What attribute of God is described here, and how is it described?

_____

_____

_____

_____

Read Exodus 34:6-7. How does God describe Himself?

_____

_____

_____

_____

_____

Read the following Scriptures and describe what characteristics of God are found in them:

Psalm 57:10

_____

_____

_____

Psalm 136:1

_____

_____

_____

Ephesians 2:4

_____

_____

_____

James 5:11

_____

_____

_____

_____

Either summarize in two or three sentences the truth in the above verses, or use phrases from these verses to write a praise song to the Lord.

_____

_____

_____

_____

_____

Read Lamentations 3:22-23. Even when we fail God, what comfort do we have in Him? Fill in the blanks:

Because of the LORD's great _____ we are not consumed, for his _____ never fail. They are new every morning.

Write the dictionary definition of "compassionate":

_____

_____

_____

_____

_____

EVIDENCE OF GOD'S MERCY
Recall a situation in your life when God's mercy was evident to you. What did God do? How did you respond?

_____

_____

_____

_____

Read Nehemiah 9:16-17,29-31. How did God evidence His merciful compassion to the Israelites when they sinned against Him?

_____

_____

_____

_____

According to Titus 3:5, how does God manifest His mercy to us? Fill in the blanks:

> He saved us, not because of _____ things we had done, but because of his _____.

RECEIVING GOD'S MERCY

We know we need God's mercy, but how can we receive it? To whom does He show His kindness and compassion? Read the following verses and note the phrases that tell to whom God extends His mercy:

Exodus 20:6

_____

_____

_____

_____

2 Chronicles 6:14

_____

_____

_____

_____

Psalm 32:10

_____

_____

_____

_____

Psalm 86:5

_____
_____
_____
_____
_____
_____

Psalm 103:11

_____
_____
_____
_____
_____
_____

Proverbs 28:13

_____
_____
_____
_____
_____
_____

Hebrews 4:16

_____
_____
_____
_____
_____
_____

Which one of the above verses is most meaningful to you? Why?

_____
_____
_____
_____

CHANNELS OF GOD'S MERCY

Read Matthew 5:7 and Luke 6:36. As a result of God's mercy to us, by what principle did Jesus instruct us to live?

_____

_____

_____

_____

_____

Why did Jesus call the merciful blessed?

_____

_____

_____

_____

_____

Read Colossians 3:12. While we are being conformed to the image of Christ, Paul tells us to "put on" certain qualities. The first Christlike quality he mentions is compassion. What does "compassion" mean to you?

_____

_____

_____

_____

_____

Give an example of someone who shows compassion to others. Tell what that person has done. Try to define the attitude in which it was done.

_____

_____

_____

_____

_____

Read Proverbs 19:17 and Zechariah 7:9-10. In what ways were God's people to show mercy to others?

_____

_____

_____

_____

_____

According to Zechariah 7:11-14, when the Israelites failed to practice such mercy, what was the result?

_____

_____

_____

_____

Do you see yourself as a judging or a merciful person?

_____

_____

_____

_____

Do you perceive judging as a sin or a right? Why?

_____

_____

_____

_____

_____

Read Deuteronomy 14:28-29 and 24:19. To whom does God expect His people to be merciful?

_____

_____

_____

_____

What will His people who are merciful receive as a result?

_____
_____
_____
_____

Why is it so important to God that we show mercy?

_____
_____
_____
_____
_____

Read 2 Corinthians 1:3-4. How is God described to His own children?

_____
_____
_____
_____
_____

For what purpose does He comfort us in our trouble?

_____
_____
_____
_____

A Closer Look at My Own Heart

We are never more beautiful or Christlike than when we reflect the mercy of God in practical ways. Read Luke 10:25-37. In this parable, Jesus gives an example of showing mercy in a practical way. Traditionally, the Jews and Samaritans hated each other. Therefore, the Jews must have been rankled that Jesus made a Samaritan the hero of this story.

Read verses 33-35 carefully, noting the compassion of the Samaritan toward one who was his enemy. (The money he paid for the injured man's lodging was probably adequate for two months.)

In verse 37, what did Jesus say to the expert in the law (and to you)?

_____

_____

_____

_____

_____

How do you think you would react if Jesus told you to show the same quality of mercy to someone you hated? Write about it in your journal. As you do, respond to the following statement: It is only by choosing to obey God's Word and by the power of the Holy Spirit that we can extend this kind of mercy to someone who has deeply wounded us or someone we love. Ask God to help you select a verse from His Word to explain your answer.

Action Steps I Can Take Today

Have you taken the mercy of God for granted? Begin now to praise Him daily for His mercy to you. Write Psalm 86:15 on an index card and place it beside your bed. Make it your morning praise song each day this week.

Ask God to make you a channel for His mercy to flow to others. Ask Him to show you a particular person to whom you can be a channel of God's comfort. Pray for that person each day this week. Ask God to show specific ways that you can comfort and/or encourage this person.

PART TWO: THE FAITHFULNESS OF GOD

God is faithful. We can count on Him to keep His Word, rely on Him to make good on His promises, depend on Him to do what He has said He will do, and trust Him to remain loving and loyal to us no matter what. God is a person upon whom we can rely absolutely. What a wonderful friend He is!

Is this an accurate description of the God you know? If not, why not?

_____

_____

_____

_____

_____

A Closer Look at the Problem

Lisa had a husband, two sons, a successful business she ran from her home, and a cabin in the woods. Listen to her story:

> Even though I had it all, it didn't satisfy. My husband bored me—
> I quit trying to meet his needs. The boys and I stopped going to
> church—I was too busy anyway. Eventually I had an affair. It didn't
> last long, but it was long enough for me to lose my husband and
> family. Even my business. I know now that I had a lot to learn
> about commitment and faithfulness. Or maybe I did know but
> just didn't want to put it into practice. Whatever, I'm just glad God
> hasn't given up on me. He's right there beside me, helping me get
> my life back on track. It hasn't been easy, but one thing I know.
> God is faithful.

Lisa learned about faithfulness the hard way. But her words attest to the faithfulness of our Lord, even in today's world where materialism is on the rise, families are in trouble, and divorce is rampant. Today, faith is rare. This lesson will help us understand more about the trustworthiness of our Lord. And that isn't all. It will also show us how to respond in faithfulness to Him and to others.

A Closer Look at God's Truth

Read Revelation 19:11. What is Christ, as the rider of the white horse, called?

_____

_____

_____

_____

_____

In the following passages, how does God show Himself to be faithful?

Deuteronomy 32:4

_____

_____

_____

_____

Isaiah 25:1

_____
_____
_____
_____
_____

Isaiah 49:7

_____
_____
_____
_____
_____

The words "faithful" and "faithfulness" come from a Hebrew word that means "to prop or support."[2] When applied to a person, it means one on whom we can safely rely. In Greek, "faithful" may be translated "trustworthy."[3]

DESCRIPTIONS OF GOD'S FAITHFULNESS
Read the following Scriptures describing the extent of God's faithfulness. Then write the reference beside the correct description.

Psalm 33:4   Psalm 36:5   Psalm 89:2   Psalm 89:8   Psalm 146:6

_____ It is established in the heavens.
_____ It reaches to the skies.
_____ Like God, it is forever.
_____ It is shown in all He does.
_____ It surrounds Him.

How can the above verses give you a sense of security?

_____
_____
_____
_____
_____
_____

God's faithfulness is boundless. Therefore, we can confidently rely on Him for all our physical, mental and spiritual needs.

GOD'S FAITHFULNESS IN ACTION

According to the following verses, what is one way that God shows His faithfulness to us?

Deuteronomy 7:9

_____
_____
_____
_____
_____

1 Kings 8:56

_____
_____
_____
_____
_____

Psalm 119:89-90

_____
_____
_____

Hebrews 10:23

_____
_____
_____

Hebrews 10:36-38

_____
_____
_____
_____

So, one way that God shows His faithfulness to us is by keeping His covenants and promises to His people. Another way God shows His faithfulness manifests itself when we are suffering.

Read 1 Peter 4:19. What should those who suffer do?

_____

_____

_____

_____

_____

When we commit ourselves to God in times of trial, He shows His faithfulness to us by delivering us in His time and way. From your personal experiences and your present knowledge of God, has He always been faithful to you? Why or why not?

_____

_____

_____

_____

If you were encouraging someone to become a Christian, could you describe God as One on whom it is safe to totally lean? What would you say?

_____

_____

_____

_____

Read 1 Corinthians 10:13. How are we assured that we are not the only ones who are being tempted?

_____

_____

_____

_____

How does God show His faithfulness to us?

_____

_____

_____

_____

What does He provide for us when we face temptation?

_____

_____

_____

_____

The original Hebrew word translated "temptation" or "testing" means "a putting to proof or an experience."[4] It implies going through adversity, a time of testing. In His faithfulness and by His grace, God does not allow His suffering children to endure more than they can handle. How can this knowledge of God's faithfulness give you comfort in your trials?

_____

_____

_____

_____

According to Psalm 119:75, in what ways does God here show His faith-fulness?

_____

_____

_____

_____

Read Hebrews 12:6,10. What does God do to those He loves and accepts as His children?

_____

_____

_____

_____

What is God's purpose for disciplining us?

_____

_____

_____

_____

Reread Lamentations 3:22-23. How are God's compassions described?

[God's] compassions never _____. They are _____ every morning; _____ is your _____.

Read 2 Timothy 2:13. If we are faithless to God, what does God do? What does that reveal about His relationship to us?

_____

_____

_____

_____

Why is this so?

_____

_____

_____

_____

What does this tell you about the nature of God? Does it give you a greater desire to be faithful to Him?

_____

_____

_____

_____

Read 1 John 1:9. If we confess our sins, what will God do?

_____

_____

_____

_____

What is God faithfully doing for us? Draw a line from each statement to its correct verse.

He strengthens and protects us.   1 Corinthians 1:8-9

He keeps us strong to the end.   1 Thessalonians 5:23-24

He sanctifies us until He comes.   2 Thessalonians 3:3

We observe the faithfulness of God in nature by the changing seasons, through history in fulfilled covenants and promises, and by experience. We see it in the Bible—the written expression of God's faithfulness to us. Read Psalm 119:86; 1 Timothy 1:15 and Revelation 21:5. Why can we totally rely upon the Word of God?

_____

_____

_____

_____

_____

A Closer Look at My Own Heart

We have seen that God is faithful and manifests that attribute to us in many ways. But He not only is faithful Himself; He also wants us, as His representatives on earth, to be faithful, too. According to each of the following verses, how are we expected to practice faithfulness?

2 Kings 12:15

_____

_____

_____

_____

2 Chronicles 34:12

_____

_____

_____

_____

Proverbs 11:13

_____

_____

_____

_____

Luke 16:10-12

_____

_____

_____

_____

Acts 17:11

_____

_____

_____

_____

1 Timothy 3:11

_____

_____

_____

_____

3 John 5

_____

_____

_____

_____

Analyze your faithfulness alongside the verses you have just read. Which areas are strong in your life?

_____

_____

_____

_____

_____

_____

Which areas need to grow?

_____

_____

_____

_____

What steps can you take now that will encourage your faithfulness to increase?

_____

_____

_____

_____

_____

Even though God has called us to faithfulness, there are times when we do not know how to make this a reality. God understands our hearts. That's why His Word abounds with encouragement for us to continue on. According to Revelation 2:10, how long are we to remain faithful?

_____

_____

_____

_____

What will be our reward for faithfulness?

_____

_____

_____

_____

Read Proverbs 28:20. What will be a result of faithfulness in our daily lives?

_____

_____

_____

_____

According to Psalm 101:6, who is God looking at?

_____

_____

_____

_____

_____

Who will minister to the end?

_____

_____

_____

_____

_____

Answer the following questions to help you discern the areas of need in your life:

When affliction comes, what attitude do I need in order to mature spiritually?

_____

_____

_____

_____

How can I be faithful even in small matters?

_____

_____

_____

_____

Am I ready to read and meditate on God's Word daily? What do I need to do to enable me to be faithful in my personal time with Him?

_____

_____

_____

Because I know that God remains faithful to me, how can I return godlike faith to a friend who disappoints me?

———————————————————————————————

———————————————————————————————

———————————————————————————————

———————————————————————————————

Action Steps I Can Take Today

God desires that we respond to His faithfulness. Read Psalms 40:10 and 89:1. Respond to these Scriptures by sharing a specific example of God's faithfulness to you. Then turn it into a song as the psalmist did in Psalm 78.

Notes

1. Alexander Pope, "The Universal Prayer," lines 37–40.
2. James Strong, *The New Strong's Exhaustive Concordance of the Bible* (Nashville, TN: Thomas Nelson Publishers, 1984), #539.
3. Ibid., #4301.
4. Ibid., #3986.

THREE

THE GOODNESS OF GOD

A loving father provides for his children. He not only supplies them with a home, food and clothing; but also, if possible, sets aside money for their future needs. Just so, our heavenly Father shows His goodness to us by providing material and spiritual blessings here on earth as well as riches in heaven.

A Closer Look at the Problem

Sometimes, especially when difficulties come, it is possible to doubt the goodness of God. Which of the following circumstances have you experienced? Put a check beside the ones that made you wonder if God was truly good.

- ❑ financial setback
- ❑ illness
- ❑ church conflict
- ❑ loss of job
- ❑ death of a loved one
- ❑ family dissension
- ❑ housing problem
- ❑ other: _____

In spite of either our feelings or our circumstances, God's Word stands firm. God is good. In this lesson we will see how His goodness is manifested to us materially and spiritually. We'll also see what our response to that goodness should be and how we can pass it on to others.

Yes, God is good, even during difficult times. It's something we need to remember and rejoice in.

A Closer Look at God's Truth

GOD'S GOODNESS

Read the following verses and complete the sentences:

    2 Chronicles 7:3:   By His very nature, God is _____.
    Psalm 31:19:   God's goodness is _____.
    Psalm 145:9:   The Lord is _____.

How have you seen the goodness of God expressed in the daily circumstances of your life? Give specific examples.

_____
_____
_____
_____
_____
_____

MATERIAL BLESSINGS

The Lord manifests His goodness, first of all, by giving us material blessings. Read the following verses and note how these blessings are described:

Psalm 21:3

_____
_____
_____

Psalm 65:11

_____
_____
_____

Psalm 68:9-10

_____
_____
_____

Jeremiah 33:9

_____

_____

_____

_____

_____

Read Matthew 5:45 and Acts 14:17. What material blessings does the Lord give us in His goodness?

_____

_____

_____

_____

_____

_____

What material blessings has God given you?

_____

_____

_____

_____

_____

_____

SPIRITUAL BLESSINGS

The Lord not only gives us bountiful material blessings but spiritual blessings as well. Read Isaiah 63:7-9. What blessings did God give to His people?

I will tell of the _____ of the LORD, the _____ for which he is to be praised . . . yes, the many _____ _____ he has done for the house of Israel. . . . In all their distress he too was _____, and the angel of his presence _____ them. In his love and mercy he _____ them; he _____ them up and carried them all the days of old.

Read Psalm 31:19-24. According to verse 19, God has stored up good things for those who _____ Him. In what other ways does God show His goodness to us?

Verse 20a

_____
_____
_____
_____
_____

Verse 20b

_____
_____
_____
_____

Verse 21

_____
_____
_____
_____

Verse 23

_____
_____
_____
_____

What other spiritual blessings have you received, including special people in your life?

_____
_____
_____
_____

How can you then respond (see verse 24)?

_____

_____

_____

_____

_____

Like a loving earthly father, God is storing up wonderful things for us in heaven and here on earth as we walk with Him. The word "bestow" in verse 19 literally means "to do or make."[1] The original Hebrew word is translated "wrought" in some Bible versions. This word means to make or do some things systematically and habitually.

It is God's practice to do good things for His children, like an earthly father who builds a go-cart for his son or a mother who paints a lovely T-shirt for her daughter. God not only habitually does good things for us, but He also does them systematically according to His time schedule and perfect plan. Our response should be one of reverence and trust. Complete the following:

> As it is written: "No eye has _____, no ear has _____,
> no mind has _____ what God has _____
> for those who _____ him" (1 Corinthians 2:9; see
> Isaiah 64:4).

In His goodness, God is preparing something for us so beyond our fondest dreams that we cannot even imagine what it will be like. No wonder we sing, "God is so good!"

FULL SATISFACTION

Another spiritual blessing God gives us out of His goodness is satisfaction. Often we try to find our satisfaction in earthly things. God shows us in His Word that that won't work. Read Psalm 107:9 and Luke 1:53. What is the main prerequisite to being satisfied with God's goodness?

_____

_____

_____

_____

_____

Read Psalm 81:8-16. Note some further conditions on our part for true satisfaction.

Verse 8

_____

_____

_____

_____

Verse 9

_____

_____

_____

_____

Verse 10

_____

_____

_____

_____

Verse 13

_____

_____

_____

_____

What results does God then promise us?

Verse 10b

_____

_____

_____

Verse 14

_____
_____
_____
_____
_____

Verse 16

_____
_____
_____
_____
_____

Read Isaiah 55:1-3. What is our spiritual condition apart from God (see verses 1-2a)?

_____
_____
_____
_____
_____

What can we do to change this condition (see verse 1)?

_____
_____
_____
_____
_____

How can we partake of God's food and drink (see verse 2b)?

_____
_____
_____
_____
_____

Read Psalm 103:5. According to this passage, what is the result of being satisfied with God's goodness?

_____

_____

_____

_____

_____

_____

Time spent with God in His Word and in prayer brings not only satisfaction but also rejuvenation in body, soul and spirit.

OUR RESPONSE
Read Psalm 103:1-5. What did David tell his soul (see verse 1)?

_____

_____

_____

_____

_____

In the light of God's goodness, what are we not to do (see verse 2)?

_____

_____

_____

_____

_____

_____

What are these benefits? Draw a line to match each benefit with the correct verse in Psalm 103.

Redemption from the pit	verse 3a
Satisfaction with good things	verse 3b
Forgiveness of sins	verse 4a
Restoration of health	verse 4b
A crown of love and compassion	verse 5

The Israelites expressed their attitude toward the goodness of God by worshiping Him (see 1 Kings 8:62-66). How can we follow their example?

_____

_____

_____

_____

Read Psalm 136:1. What are we to do?

_____

_____

_____

_____

How often do you rejoice in God's goodness?

_____

_____

_____

_____

Do you give God thanks at times other than your regular prayer time? Tell about when and how you do it.

_____

_____

_____

_____

SHOWING GOD'S GOODNESS TO OTHERS
Read the following verses, and then write after each reference how you can evidence God's goodness to others:

2 Corinthians 9:8

_____

_____

_____

_____

Galatians 6:9

_____

_____

_____

_____

Galatians 6:10

_____

_____

_____

_____

Hebrews 13:16

_____

_____

_____

_____

What are some practical ways we can show God's goodness to others? Be specific.

_____

_____

_____

_____

Read James 4:17. If we don't do good to others, what are we doing?

_____

_____

_____

_____

A Closer Look at My Own Heart

Use the following questions to help you prayerfully discern areas of need in your life.

How will understanding that God in His goodness is storing up good things for me and has a perfect plan for me change my attitudes and lifestyle?

_____

_____

_____

_____

_____

_____

How does realizing God's goodness toward me affect my attitude toward suffering and trials?

_____

_____

_____

_____

_____

Am I faithful about doing good to others? What can I improve?

_____

_____

_____

_____

_____

Action Steps I Can Take Today

Think about the aspect of God's goodness that has been most meaningful to you this past week. How can your personal expression of that particular aspect make you more like Jesus? Write about it in your journal, and then ask a friend to pray with you for this area and to keep you accountable about personally expressing God's goodness to others.

Note

1. James Strong, *The New Strong's Exhaustive Concordance of the Bible* (Nashville, TN: Thomas Nelson Publishers, 1984), #6466.

FOUR

THE WISDOM OF GOD

Our jet-black kitty likes to visit another cat across the street. However, we don't want her sauntering over there because we know a car might hit her. So we call her, go after her and scold her for her misdeed. Kitty doesn't understand why she shouldn't visit her friend. She flips her tail and fusses and fumes. But in our higher wisdom, we know best.

Similarly, our heavenly Father knows best. His wisdom is infinitely higher than ours. Since He is all-wise, He knows all things in the past, present and future. He knows how to handle every situation.

A Closer Look at the Problem

What are some of the ways that you have tried to gain wisdom?

_____

_____

_____

_____

_____

Read Colossians 2:8. What dangers are involved in trusting the world's wisdom?

_____

_____

_____

_____

_____

We are wise only when we reject our own poor wisdom and seek God's instead. This lesson will help us not to depend on our own reasoning but to trust God for the wisdom we need.

A Closer Look at God's Truth

GOD, THE ALL-WISE AND ALL-KNOWING
Read the following verses slowly and prayerfully. Allow your heart to respond to the awesome greatness of His wisdom, and describe the extent of God's knowledge and understanding.

Job 37:16

_____

_____

_____

Psalm 139:6

_____

_____

_____

Psalm 147:4-5

_____

_____

_____

Isaiah 40:28

_____

_____

_____

_____

Daniel 2:22

_____

_____

_____

Read Romans 11:33. What did Paul say about God's wisdom?

Oh, the _____ of the _____ of the _____
and _____ of God! How _____ his
_____, and his paths beyond tracing out!

Read Isaiah 55:8-9. What does God say about His thoughts and ways as compared with ours?

_____

_____

_____

_____

_____

What picture does God use to describe how different His thoughts and ways are from ours?

_____

_____

_____

_____

Since we cannot fully understand God's ways and thoughts, how then are we to pray?

_____

_____

_____

_____

Read Jeremiah 10:12. How did God use His attribute of wisdom in creation?

God made the _____ by his _____; he founded the
_____ by his _____ and stretched out the
_____ by his _____.

What does God know about us? Draw a line to match each phrase with its correct reference.

Those who are His   Psalm 103:14
Our words before we speak   Psalm 139:4
Our way   Psalm 142:3
Number of our hairs   Matthew 6:8
How we are formed   Matthew 10:30
Our hearts   Luke 16:15
What we need before we ask   2 Timothy 2:19

Our all-wise God is fully aware of everything that happens to us. Even though Satan may bring difficulty our way, God allows it only for our good. God is able to see beyond our tears to the glory that will follow. He knows our thoughts, our fears, our desires and our circumstances.

Read Exodus 3:7-10. What did God tell Moses, and what was God going to do about it?

I have indeed _____ the misery of my people in Egypt. I have _____ them crying out . . . , and I am _____ about their suffering. I have come down to _____ _____.

Read Galatians 1:15-16. Even before the apostle Paul was born, God knew what he would become in later life. How do we know this?

_____
_____
_____
_____
_____

How is this truth further emphasized in 1 Peter 1:1-2?

_____
_____
_____
_____
_____

How can these facts about God's knowledge of you help you to accept yourself?

_____

_____

_____

_____

_____

_____

JESUS, THE WISDOM OF GOD

Read John 3:16 and Ephesians 1:7-8. What is the ultimate way God has shown His wisdom to us?

_____

_____

_____

_____

_____

_____

In His life and ministry on earth, Jesus evidenced the wisdom of God. Read Isaiah 11:2. What qualities would the coming Messiah have?

The _____ of the LORD will rest on him—the Spirit of _____ and of _____, the Spirit of _____ and of power, the Spirit of _____ and of the fear of the Lord.

Read Matthew 13:54 and Luke 2:40, and explain how Isaiah's prophecy was fulfilled.

_____

_____

_____

_____

_____

_____

Read Colossians 2:2-3. What did Paul say was the genuine knowledge that
Christians have?

That they may have the full riches of complete _____,
in order that they may know the mystery of God, namely,
_____, in whom are hidden all the _____ of
_____ and _____.

We have seen that wisdom is an attribute of God the Father and His Son,
Jesus. But we also need to consider that He wants to give some of His wisdom to us, His children. But do we really need that wisdom? And if we do,
what will happen when we get it?

_____
_____
_____
_____

Read James 3:17. Describe the qualities of the wisdom that we can receive
from God.

_____
_____
_____
_____

How were these qualities evident in Jesus' life on earth? Give an example
or two.

_____
_____
_____
_____

How are they evident in your life? Explain your answer.

_____
_____
_____
_____

How do you wish they were more evident in your life?

_____

_____

_____

_____

_____

Read 1 Corinthians 1:18-31. What is Jesus to us, and how does our wisdom and strength compare to God's?

To Christians, Jesus is not only the _____ of God but also the _____ of God (see verse 24).

The foolishness of God is _____ than man's _____, and the weakness of God is _____ than man's _____ (verse 25).

Why has God chosen the following?

Foolish things (verse 27)

_____

_____

_____

_____

_____

Weak things (verse 27)

_____

_____

_____

_____

_____

Lowly, despised, and "are not" things (see verse 28)

_____

_____

_____

_____

According to verses 29 and 31, what was God's ultimate reason for choosing as He did?

_____

_____

_____

_____

_____

_____

How has the Lord worked in your life to bring you to the place of boasting only of Him?

_____

_____

_____

_____

_____

GOD'S PEOPLE, SEEKERS OF WISDOM

God chose us, not for our wisdom, might or nobility, but because we were foolish enough to believe and weak enough to trust in Him. We realize now our need of God's wisdom, but how do we go about getting it? Let's look at three different ways spoken of in the Bible: (1) reverencing God, (2) asking Him for wisdom, and (3) studying and obeying His Word.

1. *Reverencing God*

Reverence goes beyond a mere show of respect. Reverence acknowledges the unassailable superiority of the one being honored. How is this described in Psalm 111:10?

> The _____ of the LORD is the _____ of wisdom; all who follow his _____ have good _____.

Theologian J. I. Packer said, "Not till we have become humble and teachable, standing in awe of God's holiness and sovereignty, acknowledging our own littleness, distrusting our own thoughts, and willing to have our minds turned upside down, can divine wisdom become ours."[1]

2. *Asking God for His Wisdom*
Read James 1:5-6. How do we receive divine wisdom?

_____

_____

_____

_____

_____

What will God then do?

_____

_____

_____

_____

What must we do as we ask for wisdom?

_____

_____

_____

Do you find it easy to believe all that you have been taught in the Christian faith? If not, what is it that troubles you?

_____

_____

_____

_____

Do you find the principles of faith easy to believe but difficult to live? Explain your answer.

_____

_____

_____

_____

_____

Read John 14:26 and 16:13. What is the role of the Holy Spirit in regard to God's wisdom?

_____

_____

_____

_____

_____

_____

What exactly do these verses tell us? Do you believe them? Why or why not?

_____

_____

_____

_____

_____

_____

Give a specific example of how the Holy Spirit has guided you into truth.

_____

_____

_____

_____

_____

_____

3. *Studying and Obeying God's Word*
Read Colossians 3:16. What is the source of wisdom?

Let the _____ of Christ _____
in you richly as you _____ and admonish one
another with all _____.

Read 2 Timothy 3:15-16. What kind of wisdom does the Bible give us?

_____

_____

_____

_____

_____

For what is the Bible useful?

_____
_____
_____
_____
_____

What is the purpose of Bible study?

_____
_____
_____
_____
_____

A Closer Look at My Own Heart

Take some time right now and meditate on Galatians 1:15-16 and 1 Peter 1:1-2. What emotions do you feel as you ponder these verses? Joy? Doubt? Great responsibility? Fear? Write your thoughts in your journal.

Answer the following questions to help you focus even more closely on the wisdom God has for you right now:

Am I aware that God in His wisdom has a perfect plan for my life?

_____
_____
_____
_____

Do I realize that everything that happens to me has the seal of God's wisdom on it?

_____
_____
_____
_____

Do I understand why it is necessary to read God's Word and obey it?

_____

_____

_____

_____

Will I seek to speak with God-given wisdom rather than with the wisdom of the world?

_____

_____

_____

_____

Action Steps I Can Take Today

Acquiring God's wisdom begins with prayer. Personalize Ephesians 1:17-19 into your own prayer. Change "you" to "me" or "I," and change "your" to "my." ("I keep asking that the God of our Lord Jesus Christ, the glorious Father, may give [me] the Spirit of wisdom and revelation, so that [I] may know him better. . . .")

Spend time praying this same prayer for someone else. ("I keep asking that the God of our Lord Jesus Christ, the glorious Father may give [insert name] the Spirit of wisdom and revelation, so that [he or she] may know him better. . . .")

Another scriptural passage that you can adapt and pray for yourself or others is Colossians 1:9-12.

Note

1. J. I. Packer, *Knowing God* (Downers Grove, IL: InterVarsity Press, 1976), pp. 90-91.

FIVE

THE OMNIPOTENCE OF GOD

The fourth word in the Bible is the first mentioned name of God in the Bible (see Genesis 1:1). The Hebrew for this name is *Elohim;* it means mighty, strong and prominent. Creative glory, power and Godhead fullness are connected with it, as is the idea of omnipotence or governing power.[1]

A Closer Look at the Problem

God is omnipotent. That means He is all-powerful. He has unlimited authority, power and influence. With Him, nothing is impossible.

We, however, are weak and powerless. Without God, we are nothing and can do nothing worthwhile. God wants us to realize this and to put our trust completely in Him, letting Him live and work through us.

A. B. Simpson, a middle-aged Presbyterian pastor, was once physically sick, despondent and ready to quit the ministry. Then he heard someone sing, "Nothing is too hard for Jesus. No man can work like Him." After yielding himself to God, he was healed in body, mind and spirit and lived to do a great work for the Lord.

The goal of this chapter is to help us understand that we can ask for our Lord's power to do the impossible. His strength is activated within us through our weakness and dependence upon Him.

A Closer Look at God's Truth

Throughout the Old Testament, we catch glimpses of God's almighty power in His various names. Those same names are unfolded in the person of Jesus Christ and are further manifested in the revelation of who He is in the book of Revelation.

Read the following Scriptures that make known the names of God and also reveal His power:

Genesis 35:11: What does God call Himself in this verse?

_____

_____

_____

_____

Psalm 91:1: What two names are used to refer to God?

_____

_____

_____

_____

John 1:49: Who does Nathanael say Jesus is?

_____

_____

_____

Revelation 11:17: What is God called? Why is He called this?

_____

_____

_____

The Hebrew word for "almighty" is *shadday*, derived from the word meaning "to be burly, powerful, impregnable."[2] In the New Testament, the Greek word for "almighty" is *pantokrater*, "the all-ruling one (as absolute and universal sovereign)."[3] The following Scriptures tell us more about our omnipotent God:

Job 42:2: Of what was Job assured regarding God?

_____

_____

_____

Matthew 19:26: What did Jesus say about divine omnipotence?

_____

_____

_____

_____

_____

God is able to do anything. Because God has infinite power, all things are possible with Him. How does the fact of God's power encourage you in your own circumstances?

_____

_____

_____

_____

_____

GOD'S OMNIPOTENCE REVEALED IN NATURE AND IN MANKIND
The first way that God's omnipotence is revealed is in His control of nature. Read Psalm 33:6-9 and note the various aspects of God's power in creation.

Verse 6:
By the word of the LORD were the _____ _____,
their _____ _____ by the breath of his mouth.

Verse 7:
He gathers the _____ of the _____ _____ _____;
he puts the _____ into _____.

Verse 9:
He spoke, and ____ _____ ___ ____; he commanded, and ____
_____ _____.

Read Amos 4:13. What things in nature does God control?

He who forms the _____, creates the _____, and
reveals his _____ to man, he who turns _____ to

darkness, and treads the _____ _____ of the earth—the
_____ _____ _____ is his name.

Why do you think there are earthquakes, tornadoes and floods? Are they
only indicators of God's power? Or are they evidence of creation out of
control?

_____
_____
_____
_____
_____
_____

Are these disasters sent to bring frightened people to salvation? What other
possible reasons are there for these powerful displays of God's power?

_____
_____
_____
_____
_____

Do we have the right or authority through prayer and the spoken word of
faith to challenge or change weather conditions? Why or why not?

_____
_____
_____
_____

Not only is nature controlled by God's power, but men also are subject to
His will. This also includes leaders of nations. Read Daniel 2:20-21 and
4:25. What belongs to the omnipotent God (see Daniel 2:20)?

_____
_____
_____
_____

What things is God able to do to nations?

> He changes _____ and _____, he sets up _____
> and _____ them. He gives wisdom to the _____
> and knowledge to the _____ (Daniel 2:21).

What are some other ways in which God controls nations?

_____
_____
_____
_____
_____
_____

Do we even need to vote? Complete this statement: "We vote because God uses men to . . ."

_____
_____
_____
_____
_____
_____

GOD CONTROLS ANGELS BY HIS OMNIPOTENT POWER
Read Hebrews 1:14. What are angels called?

_____
_____
_____
_____

What are they commissioned to do?

_____
_____
_____
_____
_____

What are some specific ways that angels minister to people today?

_____

_____

_____

_____

_____

SATAN AND DEMONS ARE UNDER GOD'S OMNIPOTENT CONTROL
According to Job 1:12; 2:3-6, God told Satan he could go only so far in afflicting Job. Where did God draw the line?

_____

_____

_____

_____

_____

In your view, is God always in complete control, or does the enemy's power sometimes come dangerously close to winning the battle?

_____

_____

_____

_____

Read Mark 1:23-28. How did Jesus deal with the unclean spirit?

_____

_____

_____

_____

Why were people amazed at Jesus?

_____

_____

_____

_____

As we grow more like Jesus, can we expect to exercise His kind of power over demons and sickness? Why or why not?

_____

_____

_____

_____

_____

GOD'S AUTHORITY OVER SICKNESS AND DEATH

Read Matthew 8:14-17. How did Jesus minister to Peter's mother-in-law (see verses 14-15)?

_____

_____

_____

_____

_____

Notice the extent of Jesus' healing ministry, described in verse 16. What Old Testament Scripture did He fulfill (see verse 17)?

_____

_____

_____

_____

_____

Read John 10:17-18 and 11:43-44. What authority did Jesus have over death?

_____

_____

_____

_____

How did He reveal this authority in the case of Lazarus?

_____

_____

_____

_____

Our Response to God's Omnipotence

So, how are we to respond to God's omnipotence? First, God wants us to trust Him for impossible situations in our lives, and then He wants us to depend on Him entirely.

Read Luke 1:26-55. What promise did God give Mary through the angel Gabriel (see verse 31)?

_____

_____

_____

_____

_____

_____

What further aspects of this promise are described in verses 32 and 33?

He will be _____ and will be called the _____ of the _____ _____. The Lord God will give him the _____ of his father David, and he will reign over the _____ of Jacob forever; his kingdom will _____ _____.

What honest question did Mary have (see verse 34)?

_____

_____

_____

_____

_____

_____

What did Gabriel say to Mary that explained how God's promise was to be fulfilled (see verses 35-36)?

The Holy Spirit will _____ _____ you, and the power of the Most High will _____ you. So the holy one to be born will be called the _____ of _____. Even Elizabeth your relative is going to have a _____ in her old age, and she who was said to be barren is in her _____ month.

What affirmation did Gabriel give Mary (see verse 37)?

_____

_____

_____

Verse 37 could be translated literally, "No word will be impossible of fulfillment with God." The *Amplified Bible* says, "For with God nothing is ever impossible and no word from God shall be without power or impossible of fulfillment."

God used an old woman (Elizabeth) to give birth to the prophet John the Baptist, and a virgin (Mary) to give birth to His Son, Jesus. Elizabeth had a barren womb and Mary was a virgin. Both women faced impossible situations. Yet out of these human impossibilities, God brought forth life "so that no one may boast before him" (1 Corinthians 1:29).

What was Mary's response to God's promise (see Luke 1:38)?

_____

_____

_____

_____

Share a promise God has given you and how He has fulfilled it. If it hasn't yet been fulfilled, explain how you believe He will do so in the future.

_____

_____

_____

The second way we can respond to God's omnipotence is by depending on Him entirely. Read 2 Chronicles 14. King Asa decided to follow the Lord fully. List the things Asa did in obedience to God.

Verse 2

_____

_____

_____

Verse 3

_____

_____

_____

_____

Verse 4

_____

_____

_____

_____

Verse 5

_____

_____

_____

_____

What difficulty did Asa then face (see verse 9)?

_____

_____

_____

_____

What was Asa's powerful prayer (see verse 11)? Fill in the blanks:

LORD, there is no one like _____ to help the _____ against the _____. Help us, O LORD our God, for we _____ on you, and in your _____ we have come _____ this _____ _____. O LORD, you are our _____; do not let man _____ against _____.

How did God answer Asa's prayer (see verses 12-13)?

_____

_____

_____

_____

_____

The Omnipotence of God   75

Read 2 Corinthians 12:9-10. The Lord said to Paul:

My _____ is sufficient for you, for my _____
is made perfect in _____.

What did Paul boast in? Why?

_____

_____

_____

_____

Paul said, "For when I am _____, then I am _____."
Paul's statement is a paradox. What does he mean?

_____

_____

_____

A Closer Look at My Own Heart

What is God saying to you? As you carefully read the following questions,
ask God to show you what step He wants you to take in response to what
you have learned about His omnipotence.

How can the fact of God's omnipotence encourage me in my own
difficult circumstances?

_____

_____

_____

Am I willing to believe and trust Him in what seems like impossible situations in my life? Why or why not?

_____

_____

_____

_____

Am I willing to depend upon His strength for my weakness? Why or why not?

_____

_____

_____

_____

How can my deepened understanding of my omnipotent God transform me more into the likeness of Jesus Christ?

_____

_____

_____

_____

In what ways can my deepened understanding change my attitude toward my weaknesses? Toward the weaknesses of others?

_____

_____

_____

_____

Action Steps I Can Take Today

God is ever ready to put forth His power for you and those you love. In your journal, write a prayer expressing the areas in your life in which you feel you need to experience God's omnipotence. Also tell God why you need more of Him in these areas.

Notes

1. James Strong, *The New Strong's Exhaustive Concordance of the Bible* (Nashville, TN: Thomas Nelson Publishers, 1984), Hebrew #430.
2. Ibid., Hebrew #7703.
3. Ibid., Hebrew #3841.

${\mathcal{T}}$HE HOLINESS OF GOD

God is holy because He is absolutely pure, good and righteous. He has no sin; in fact, He hates sin. He is majestic and far above any of His creatures (see 1 Samuel 2:2; Psalm 86:8-10; Isaiah 40:25; Hosea 11:9; 1 Timothy 6:15-16).

A Closer Look at the Problem

Obviously, for us to be holy, as He is holy, would take an act of God. And it did. Hebrews 10:10 says, "We have been made holy through the sacrifice of the body of Jesus Christ once for all."

It is incredible that a holy God would share His holiness with us as He prepares us to live with Him in heaven. But He does. As someone has well said:

> Holiness means the most utter faithfulness, the most transparent truthfulness, the most decided honesty. It means every word you speak is perfectly true. You never flatter nor slander nor try to convey a false impression; you are all through alike in business, religion, and home life. It means you set yourself to bring every thought into harmony with the will of God. It means you do to others as you wish to be done by. It means the purest chastity.

This chapter will help us see that even though holiness seems lofty and unattainable to us, through the power of Jesus' blood we can be holy as God is holy.

A Closer Look at God's Truth

GOD IS HOLY

What does the Bible tell us about the holiness of God? Draw a line to match each statement with its correct reference.

The Lord "is holy."	Exodus 15:11
God is "majestic in holiness."	Psalm 22:3
"Holy is the Lord God Almighty."	Psalm 99:9
He "will show himself holy."	Isaiah 5:16
He is "enthroned as the Holy One."	Revelation 4:8

Holiness is inherent in God's nature.

JESUS IS HOLY

What does the Bible say about the holiness of Jesus? Draw a line to match each statement to its correct reference.

He is the "Holy and Righteous One."	Luke 1:35
He is "the Holy One of God."	Luke 4:34
He is the "holy servant Jesus."	Acts 3:14
He is "the holy one to be born."	Acts 4:30

Jesus did not become holy on earth; holiness was inherent in His nature. He shares the nature of God because He is God, the second person of the Trinity. According to Scripture, why was Christ holy while on earth? Match each reference with its correct reason.

He "had no sin."	2 Corinthians 5:21
He "offered himself unblemished."	Hebrews 4:15
He was "holy, blameless, pure."	Hebrews 7:26
He was "a lamb without blemish or defect."	Hebrews 9:14
He "was without sin."	1 Peter 1:19

The Scriptures we have read have revealed the fact of the holiness of God and of His Son, Jesus. But just what does the word "holy" mean? Ask God to give you understanding of this word, and write down what you think "holy" means.

_____

_____

_____

_____

_____

_____

GOD MANIFESTS HIS HOLINESS TO MANKIND
How does God manifest His holiness?

Genesis 6:5-7

_____
_____
_____
_____

Psalm 5:4-6

_____
_____
_____
_____

Mark 9:2-4

_____
_____
_____

John 3:16

_____
_____
_____
_____

GOD DESIRES FOR HIS PEOPLE TO BE HOLY
God desires the same fellowship with men and women that He once had
with Adam and Eve in the garden. Read Isaiah 57:15. Even though God is
holy and exalted, where may He be found?

_____
_____
_____
_____
_____

Who are the contrite and lowly in spirit?

_____
_____
_____
_____
_____

Read Exodus 19:6 and Deuteronomy 7:6. How does God describe the Israelites?

_____
_____
_____
_____
_____

Read Leviticus 19:2. What does God command His people to do?

_____
_____
_____
_____
_____

Israel was the nation chosen by God to fulfill His purposes in the world. The nation of Israel was holy in the sense that it was set apart for God. But now God commands His people to act in a holy manner, to live holy lives.

Read Leviticus 18:3-4. By what means was Israel to exhibit holiness? Fill in the blanks:

You must _____ ___ as they do in _____ . . . and you must _____ ___ as they do in the land of _____, where I am bringing you. Do not _____ their _____. You must _____ my ____ and be careful to _____ my _____.

God designed moral, ceremonial and legal requirements so that Israel might be a holy people in deed as well as in fact.

Read 1 Peter 1:15-16. As God spoke to the Israelites centuries ago, what is His will for us today?

_____
_____
_____
_____
_____

Why?

_____
_____
_____
_____
_____

God does not say that we should be *as* holy as He is, for that is impossible, but He wants to share some of His holy nature with us. How can we live holy lives in an unholy world?

_____
_____
_____
_____
_____

GOD MAKES US HOLY
God makes us holy in three ways: (1) He chooses us to serve, (2) He cleanses us, and (3) He disciplines us.

First, He chooses us to serve. Read 1 Peter 2:9-10. List the five names God gives to those who believe on His Son. Compare these names with God's description of the Israelites in Exodus 19:6 and Deuteronomy 7:6.

_____
_____
_____
_____

Read Ephesians 1:4. What was God's plan for us when He chose us, even before the creation of the world?

_____

_____

_____

_____

_____

According to the following verses, how are we to serve our Holy God?

    Luke 1:74-75

    _____

    _____

    _____

    _____

    Hebrews 12:14

    _____

    _____

    _____

    _____

Reread Hebrews 12:14 and read 2 Peter 3:10-13. Why is it important that we live holy lives?

_____

_____

_____

_____

God is absolutely pure and holy. Therefore, He wants us to be holy, too. His desire is to have fellowship with us. According to Colossians 1:13, what has God done so that we can be holy?

_____

_____

_____

_____

According to 1 John 1:9, what are we to do to become holy and pure?

_____
_____
_____
_____
_____
_____

What then will God do?

_____
_____
_____
_____

The second way that God makes us holy is by cleansing us to serve Him. An example of this process of cleansing is found in an incident in the prophet Isaiah's life. Read Isaiah 6:1-8 and briefly describe the scene Isaiah saw.

_____
_____
_____
_____

What were seraphs saying about God?

_____
_____
_____
_____

How did Isaiah feel about himself?

_____
_____
_____
_____
_____

How was Isaiah's sin cleansed?

_____

_____

_____

_____

_____

_____

_____

Once we see God in His awesome holiness, we see our wretched sinful-
ness. As we confess and forsake our sin, our fellowship with God is re-
stored. It is only when we are pure before Him that can we be of service to
Him. God has also given us His Word for our cleansing (see Ephesians
5:26). We are spiritually cleansed as we read, study, meditate, memorize
and obey God's holy Word, the Bible. It is our "bath," cleansing us from
living in a defiled world.

Read 2 Peter 1:3-4. How has God equipped us to share in His divine nature?

His _____ _____ has given us _____
we need for life and _____ through our _____
of him.

What is our means of becoming holy? Fill in the blanks:

He has given us his very _____ and precious _____,
so that through _____ you may participate in the _____
_____ and _____ the _____ in the
_____ caused by evil desires.

How have you experienced the power of God's Word to change you?

_____

_____

_____

_____

_____

_____

_____

The third way that God makes us holy is by disciplining us. Read Hebrews 12:10-11 and describe what this passage states about God's discipline.

_____

_____

_____

_____

What will be the result of such discipline?

_____

_____

_____

_____

WE GAIN MUCH BY BEING MADE HOLY
What are some of the results of being made holy? (Note that the word "sanctified" in some of these passages, when it applies to us, is another word for holiness.)

Matthew 5:8

_____

_____

_____

Acts 20:32

_____

_____

_____

Romans 6:22

_____

_____

_____

2 Timothy 2:21

_____

_____

_____

_____

Hebrews 2:11

_____

_____

_____

Hebrews 10:14

_____

_____

_____

A Closer Look at My Own Heart

What is God saying to you? Carefully read the following questions. Ask God to show you what steps He wants you to take in response to what you have learned about His holiness—about His expectation that you be His holy child.

Am I a person "of unclean lips" (Isaiah 6:5)? What sins must I confess and forsake?

_____

_____

_____

Am I "contrite and lowly in spirit" (Isaiah 57:15)? If not, will I confess my pride and ask for God's forgiveness?

_____

_____

_____

Do I regularly read and meditate on God's Word? Why or why not?

_____

_____

_____

_____

_____

Do I accept God's discipline in my life?

_____

_____

_____

_____

_____

Do I ask God to help me be holy in thought, word and deed?

_____

_____

_____

_____

_____

Action Steps I Can Take Today

Complete the following sentence: "The step of action I feel God wants me to take today in response to His holiness is . . ."

_____

_____

_____

_____

_____

_____

Ask a friend to keep you accountable to what you have chosen to do.

Paraphrase 1 Thessalonians 5:23-24 into a prayer for yourself and then into a prayer for someone else. Claim the promise in verse 24 for both of you.

SEVEN

THE GRACE OF GOD

Grace is often defined as God's unmerited favor toward man. A simple acrostic will help you understand and remember what grace is:

> **G**od's
> **R** iches
> **A** t
> **C** hrist's
> **E** xpense

In His great kindness, God bestows benefits on undeserving humankind. A. W. Tozer said, "It is by His grace that God imputes merit where none previously existed and declares no debt to be where one has been before."[1]

A Closer Look at the Problem

To illustrate the magnitude of grace, Jesus told a story of a king who forgave a servant for a debt of what today would be millions of dollars. The servant, however, refused to extend that same type of grace to a fellow servant who owed him our equivalent of just a few dollars. In fact, instead of forgiving him, he had the fellow servant thrown in jail (see Matthew 18:23-35).

We read this story and wonder: *How could the servant be so ungrateful and unforgiving when he had just been treated so graciously and mercifully?* But wait. Haven't we who have been forgiven by our Lord and Master acted in similar ways toward others?

This chapter will not only show how God's marvelous grace is extended to us, but it will also help us understand how we can express that same grace to others.

A Closer Look at God's Truth

GOD IS GRACIOUS

The Lord is a God of grace and compassion. Read Exodus 34:6. What does God call Himself?

_____

_____

_____

_____

_____

Nehemiah said almost the same thing in Nehemiah 9:17. According to the last sentence in this verse, exactly how did Nehemiah describe God?

_____

_____

_____

_____

JESUS IS GRACIOUS

Just as the Lord is a God of grace and compassion, so is Jesus. How is Jesus described in the following verses?

Psalm 45:2

_____

_____

_____

Luke 2:40

_____

_____

_____

Luke 4:22

_____

_____

_____

John 1:14

_____
_____
_____
_____

THE HOLY SPIRIT IS GRACIOUS
Finally, just as Jesus is full of grace, so too is the Holy Spirit. Read Hebrews 10:29. How is the Holy Spirit described?

_____
_____
_____
_____
_____

Read Zechariah 12:10. How does God describe His Spirit in this passage?

_____
_____
_____
_____
_____

A DESCRIPTION OF GOD'S GRACE
How is God's grace described in the following verses?

Romans 5:17

_____
_____
_____

2 Corinthians 12:9

_____
_____
_____
_____

Ephesians 1:6

_____

_____

_____

_____

Ephesians 1:7

_____

_____

_____

_____

Put into your own words your understanding of what God's grace is.

_____

_____

_____

_____

How does God's grace relate to you personally?

_____

_____

_____

_____

THE BENEFITS OF GOD'S GRACE

God shows His grace to us in several ways. First of all, He saves us by His grace. Read Ephesians 2:1-3. What was our spiritual condition before His grace was exercised in our lives?

_____

_____

_____

_____

Read Titus 2:11. What does the grace of God bring?

_____
_____
_____
_____
_____
_____

To how many people has grace been made available?

_____
_____
_____
_____
_____

Read Titus 3:5-7. By what are we now justified?

_____
_____
_____
_____
_____
_____

Why did God justify us?

_____
_____
_____
_____
_____

Restate Ephesians 2:8-9 in your own words.

_____
_____
_____
_____
_____

What one ingredient must we have in order to appropriate God's grace for our salvation?

_____

_____

_____

_____

_____

Exodus 33:19 in the *Amplified Bible* says, "And God said, I will make all My goodness pass before you, and I will proclaim My name, THE LORD, before you; for I will be gracious to whom I will be gracious, and will show mercy and loving-kindness on whom I will show mercy and loving-kindness." What fact concerning His sovereignty does God make clear?

_____

_____

_____

_____

_____

God is free to do as He pleases. He does not have to forgive our sins and save us, but He chooses to do so. How does this make you feel?

_____

_____

_____

_____

_____

Although God offers salvation to every person, why do only some receive it?

_____

_____

_____

_____

_____

Not only does God give us salvation by His grace, but He also keeps giving many blessings to us throughout our earthly lives as Christians and on into eternity. What do the following verses tell us about the benefits that God has given us by His grace?

2 Corinthians 8:9

_____
_____
_____
_____
_____

2 Corinthians 12:9

_____
_____
_____
_____

Galatians 1:15

_____
_____
_____
_____
_____

2 Thessalonians 2:16

_____
_____
_____
_____

2 Timothy 2:1

_____
_____
_____
_____

Hebrews 4:16

_____
_____
_____
_____
_____

Hebrews 13:9

_____
_____
_____
_____
_____

Can you remember a time when God gave you special grace during an especially difficult time? Tell about it.

_____
_____
_____
_____
_____

Read Proverbs 3:34. To whom is God's grace given?

_____
_____
_____
_____
_____

Read Ephesians 2:8-9. Why is it impossible for grace to operate in our lives if we try to earn it by works?

_____
_____
_____
_____
_____

Grace then is the sovereign favor of God giving eternal life and showering blessings on those who do not earn or deserve it in any way. What other benefits does the Lord give us as believers besides those already mentioned?

_____
_____
_____
_____
_____

EXPRESSING GOD'S GRACE TO OTHERS
Read 2 Corinthians 1:12. How does God want us to conduct ourselves?

_____

_____

_____

_____

_____

What does Paul call us in Ephesians 2:10?

_____

_____

_____

_____

What were we created to do?

_____

_____

_____

_____

What kind of good works are we to do?

_____

_____

_____

_____

According to Philippians 2:13, who actually performs the good works through us?

_____

_____

_____

_____

Colossians 3:16-17 tells us that good works are to be performed in Christ's name with a heart of thanksgiving. What practical works that you can do are listed here?

_____

_____

_____

_____

_____

According to John 15:8, what should be the end result of every good work?

_____

_____

_____

_____

_____

Read Ephesians 4:29,32 and 1 Peter 4:10. According to these verses, how are we to minister the grace of God to others?

> [Say] only what is _____ for _____ others _____ according to their _____, that it may _____ those who _____ (Ephesians 4:29).

> Be _____ and _____ to one another, _____ each other, just as in Christ God _____ you (Ephesians 4:32).

> Each one should _____ whatever _____ he has _____ to _____ others, _____ administering God's _____ in its various forms (1 Peter 4:10).

Read 1 Peter 4:9,11.What spiritual gifts can we use to minister God's grace to others?

_____

_____

_____

_____

_____

What additional spiritual gifts are mentioned in Romans 12:6-8?

_____
_____
_____

What spiritual gifts has God given to you?

_____
_____
_____

How are you using your spiritual gifts to serve God's kingdom? If you are not using your spiritual gifts, explain why you aren't doing so.

_____
_____
_____

How do you feel now that you know that God actually planned to give you these gifts before the world began?

_____
_____
_____

God wants us to use the spiritual gifts that He has given to us, and He also gives us one other gift at which we should excel. Read 2 Corinthians 8:7 and 9:6-8. Paul urged the Corinthian believers to excel in what other grace?

We should give generously and _____.

How will God repay us when we give to those in need and in His service?

_____
_____
_____

A Closer Look at My Own Heart

Use the following questions to help you prayerfully discern areas in your own heart that need a touch of God's grace.

Now that I understand the meaning of grace, what will my attitude be toward those I come in contact with each day?

_____

_____

_____

_____

Do the good deeds I do glorify God or myself? What is to be my attitude when I do good works?

_____

_____

_____

_____

What attitude or behavior do I need to repent of in order that God's grace can be expressed in me?

_____

_____

_____

_____

Action Steps I Can Take Today

Write Ephesians 2:10 on an index card. Have you discovered the good works God has planned for you to do? Ask God to show you what they are. Be alert for opportunities to actually do those things He lays on your heart.

Note

1. A. W. Tozer, *The Knowledge of the Holy: The Attributes of God: Their Meaning in the Christian Life* (New York: Harper and Row, 1961), p. 100.

$\mathcal{T}$HE LOVE OF GOD

Love is the essence of God's nature. Not only *does* He love, but He also *is* love and the source of all love. His love is unchanging, free, spontaneous and undeserved. In the New Testament, *agape*, one of four Greek words for love, is used over three hundred times. It expresses the highest type of love—divine love.

A Closer Look at the Problem

As we receive God's love, He wants us to love Him in return and then pass His love on to others. Someone has said:

> God is the source of love,
> Christ is the proof of love,
> Service is the expression of love.

But how do we experience this love? How do we pass it on to others? Not only will this chapter focus on the varied aspects of God's love, but it will also help us understand how we can express that love to those around us.

Have you ever known or read about someone who demonstrated love by the things he or she said and/or did? Briefly describe the incident.

_____

_____

_____

_____

_____

_____

_____

_____

A Closer Look at God's Truth

Like many of God's attributes, His love is beyond our human scope of understanding. Read 1 John 4:8,16. What do these verses tell us about the character of God?

_____

_____

_____

_____

_____

_____

God's love is described in various ways in Scripture. Write each reference beside the corresponding description of His love:

Jeremiah 31:3   Romans 5:8   Ephesians 2:4   Ephesians 3:18

_____   Great
_____   Immeasurable
_____   Everlasting
_____   Sacrificial

To whom has God chosen to manifest His amazing love? List the recipients of God's love from the following verses:

Matthew 3:17

_____

_____

_____

_____

John 3:16

_____

_____

_____

_____

John 14:21

_____
_____
_____
_____

John 16:27

_____
_____
_____
_____

Romans 5:8

_____
_____
_____

As the second person in the godhead, Jesus has the same divine love as the Father. Whom does Jesus love? Draw a line from each person or group that Jesus loves to the correct reference.

Believers   John 13:1
His own disciples   John 14:31
The Father   Ephesians 5:2
The Church   Ephesians 5:25

EXPRESSIONS OF GOD'S LOVE
According to the following verses, in what ways does God the Father show His love to us?

Isaiah 49:15

_____
_____
_____
_____

Isaiah 63:9

_____

_____

_____

_____

Zephaniah 3:17

_____

_____

_____

_____

Ephesians 2:4-5

_____

_____

_____

_____

Hebrews 12:6

_____

_____

_____

_____

1 John 3:1

_____

_____

_____

1 John 4:9-10

_____

_____

_____

_____

In what ways does God the Son demonstrate His love for us? Draw a line to match each statement with its correct reference.

He makes us conquerors.	Luke 19:10
He became poor so we could be rich.	Romans 8:37
He disciplines us.	2 Corinthians 8:9
He came to save the lost.	Hebrews 7:25
He intercedes for us.	Revelation 1:5
He frees us from sin.	Revelation 3:19

Which item listed above is most meaningful to you right now? Why?

_____

_____

_____

_____

_____

God's ultimate manifestation of His love for us was His allowing Jesus to die for us—God sacrificed His own Son because He loves us. Think about the deep love that you have for your own children, family members or a special friend, and then reflect on the Father's sacrifice in giving His only Son to die for you. Would you be willing to die for someone you love? Why or why not?

_____

_____

_____

_____

_____

Would you be willing to allow your child or another person you love to go to a mission field in a foreign country if God directed him or her there? Why or why not?

_____

_____

_____

_____

RESPONSES TO GOD'S LOVE

How do we respond to God's amazing love? Do you think that we can really love the way God loves? Why or why not?

_____

_____

_____

_____

_____

First John 4:11 in the *Amplified Bible* says, "Beloved, if God loved us so [very much], we also ought to love one another" (1 John 4:11). What do the following verses say about how or why we can love others as God loves them?

Romans 5:5

_____

_____

_____

_____

1 Timothy 1:14

_____

_____

_____

_____

2 Timothy 1:7

_____

_____

_____

_____

How can we demonstrate our love for God? As you examine the verses in the following table, write what God says to do and one practical way to show it in your daily life.

Put a check mark in front of the ones you already engage in. Put an asterisk in front of the ones that you feel need to have a higher priority in your life.

Passage	What to Do	How to Show Love
Psalm 97:10	*Hate evil*	*Stop lying*
Matthew 25:34-40		
1 John 2:15		
1 John 4:20-21		
1 John 5:3		

LOVING OUR NEIGHBORS

Read Matthew 22:36-40. According to Jesus, what two all-inclusive commands sum up all the Law?

"Love the Lord your God with all your _____ and with all your _____ and with all your _____." This is the _____ and _____ commandment. And the second is _____ it: "Love your _____ as _____."

Read the following short poem by C. W. Vanderbergh:

To love the whole world
    For me is no chore;
My only problem's
    My neighbor next door.

Do you agree with the author of this poem? Why or why not?

_____

_____

_____

_____

_____

_____

God says that we are to love God and to love our neighbor. According to the following passages, who specifically is our neighbor?

Matthew 5:44

_____

_____

_____

_____

John 15:12

_____

_____

_____

_____

Ephesians 1:15

_____

_____

_____

_____

Ephesians 5:25

_____

_____

_____

_____

1 Thessalonians 3:12

_____

_____

_____

_____

Titus 2:4

_____

_____

_____

_____

In other words, *everyone* is our neighbor! Notice the type of love God wants us to have for our neighbor. Draw a line from each description of love to its correct reference.

Active, true love	John 15:13
Deep love	Romans 12:9
Sacrificial love	Philippians 1:9
Abounding love	1 Peter 4:8
Sincere love	1 John 3:18

THE GOVERNING PRINCIPLE OF GOD'S LOVE
Read 1 Corinthians 13. Even if you give all your possessions to the poor and you suffer martyrdom, what will happen if you don't have God's love?

_____

_____

_____

_____

C. I. Scofield says, "Gifts are good, but only if ministered in love."[1] Review 1 Corinthians 13:4-7, and then complete the following chart:

What love is	What love is not/does not do

What three gifts of the Spirit will remain forever (see verse 13)?

_____

_____

_____

Which gift is greatest of all?

_____

_____

_____

A Closer Look at My Own Heart

Read the following verses, and then write down some of the ways in which you can show the love of God to others:

Galatians 5:13

_____

_____

_____

_____

Galatians 6:2

_____

_____

_____

_____

Galatians 6:10

_____

_____

_____

_____

Ephesians 4:32

_____

_____

_____

_____

Philippians 2:4

_____

_____

_____

_____

1 John 3:17-18

_____

_____

_____

_____

Carefully reread the list you just made. Go back through the list and write
one or two specific ways you can put each command into practice.

John Haggai once said, "Love is . . . slow to suspect—quick to trust, slow to
condemn—quick to justify, slow to expose—quick to shield, slow to repri-
mand—quick to forbear, slow to belittle—quick to appreciate, slow to de-
mand—quick to give, slow to provoke—quick to help, slow to resent—quick
to forgive." Consider the following questions:

Do I love the Lord enough to give Him time each day—to read His
Word, to pray to Him, and to praise and love Him?

_____

_____

_____

_____

Do I love Him enough to obey His commands?

_____

_____

_____

_____

Do I show His love to my family, friends and even those who do wrong
to me?

_____

_____

_____

_____

_____

What changes will I make in my life as a result of this study?

_____

_____

_____

_____

Action Steps I Can Take Today

Pray the following prayer as an action step that you can take right now:

> *Lord, You are holy, powerful and majestic, yet You invite me,*
> *Your child, to come into Your presence. I long to be conformed into Your*
> *image, to be like You, but I know now that this process has only just*
> *begun. It will only be perfected as I get to know You better and trust your*
> *Holy Spirit at work in me. Teach me Your Word. Help me to listen, obey*
> *and show Your love to others. I love You and praise You. You are*
> *altogether lovely. In Jesus' name, I pray. Amen.*

List some practical ways you can show love to others this week. Choose one and make a commitment to do it.

_____

_____

_____

_____

_____

As you complete this study, remember that you are born to be like Jesus. And this is our prayer for you:

> *That your love may abound more and more in knowledge*
> *and depth of insight, so that you may be able to discern what is best*
> *and may be pure and blameless until the day of Christ, filled with*
> *the fruit of righteousness that comes through Jesus Christ—to the*
> *glory and praise of God* [Philippians 1:9-11].

Note

1. C. I. Scofield, *Oxford NIV Scofield Study Bible* (New York: Oxford University Press, 1984), note to 1 Corinthians 13.

CAPTIVATED BY GOD LEADER'S GUIDE

The purpose of this leader's guide is to provide those willing to lead a group Bible study with additional material to make the study more effective. Each lesson has one or two exercises designed to increase participation and lead the group members into closer relationship with their heavenly Father.

Each of the exercises is designed to introduce the study and emphasize the theme of the chapter. When two exercises are suggested, it is up to your discretion whether to use them both. Time will probably be the deciding factor.

If the group is larger than six members, you may want to break into smaller groups for the discussion time so that all will have an adequate opportunity to share. As the lessons proceed, the exercises will invite more personal sharing. Keep these two important points in mind:

1. Involve each member of the group in the discussion when at all possible. Some may be too shy or new to the Bible study experience. Be sensitive to their needs and encourage them to answer simple questions that do not require personal information or biblical knowledge. As they get more comfortable in the group, they will probably share more often.

2. Make a commitment with the group members that what is shared in the discussion times and prayer requests must be kept in strictest confidence.

After each lesson, be prepared to pray with those who have special needs or concerns. Emphasize the truth of God's Word as you minister to the group members, which will lead them to a closer relationship with their Lord and Savior.

ONE

OUR LIKENESS TO GOD

Objective

To help group members understand what it means to become more like Christ and how that transformation takes place.

Preparation

EXERCISE 1

Obtain several pieces of 9" x 12" colored construction paper or colored printer paper (at least two pieces for each group member), transparent tape (or tacks) and several felt-tip pens. You will need to clear some wall space or a bulletin board in the meeting room.

EXERCISE 2

During the week, contact group members and ask them to bring a photo of another family member that they look the most alike. If they state they don't have such a photo, ask them to think of a characteristic that they share with another family member. If you plan on doing the option of displaying the photos, you will need a poster board, wall space or bulletin board and tape.

DISCUSSION

Familiarize yourself with the questions in the following "Group Participation" section, and choose which questions you definitely want to discuss with the group. Note that there might not be time to discuss every question, so modify or adapt this discussion guide to fit the needs of your group. Additional discussion questions/action steps are provided to stimulate further discussion if you have the time. In addition, obtain 3" x 5" index cards and pens or pencils for the concluding activity.

Group Participation

Exercise 1

Give each group member at least two pieces of construction paper and a felt-tip pen. Instruct the members to write an attribute of God on each piece of paper. Give them about a minute, and then invite each member to tape or tack their two words on the wall or bulletin board. Read the many attributes and discuss which attributes of God are ones that we can gain as we become more Christlike (e.g., love, patience, kindness) and which we can never attain (e.g., omnipotence, Creator, omnipresence). State that in today's session they will explore what it means to become more like Jesus.

Exercise 2

Invite those who brought photos to share them. Allow group members a minute to look at the photos to see if they see the resemblance. As an option, you might want to display the photos on a poster board, wall or bulletin board without revealing the people who brought them. Allow members to study the photos and decide who in the group each photo resembles. (Caution: Do not put tape or use pins on the photos without the owners' permission!)

Discuss what other characteristics or mannerisms they might share with a family member. Relate this to the characteristics that we share with our heavenly Father. Discuss how we can see God's character reflected in the lives of His followers.

Discussion

1. Discuss the following questions (or the ones you have chosen) from the "A Closer Look at God's Truth" section:

   - According to Romans 8:28-29, what is one of God's great purposes for redeeming us?

   - According to Philippians 1:6, how long does this process of conforming take? What is the role of the Holy Spirit in conforming us to the likeness of Christ?

   - Read Romans 8:16-1. What is the Spirit-led believer's relationship to God? What is the ultimate goal of being led by the Spirit and conformed to Christ's image?

- What must we experience before sharing His glory? In what ways do we share in Christ's suffering?

- What does suffering accomplish in our lives? What does suffering ultimately prepare us for according to 2 Timothy 2:12? How have you experienced the process of suffering in preparing and maturing you to be more Christlike?

- According to Romans 12:1-2, what must we do to grow into Christ's likeness? How might this be related to the suffering we must endure?

- Review Moses' mountaintop experience with God described in Exodus 34:1-10. What did God reveal to Moses about Himself?

- Read 2 Corinthians 3:7-18, and compare the glory Moses received with that which we have available through Christ. Why don't we always have His radiance on our faces?

2. Discuss the following questions (or the ones you have chosen) from the "A Closer Look at My Own Heart" section:

- In order to become more Christlike, we need to spend time with Him. In what ways can we spend more time with Him?

- Summarize Mark 1:35; 6:46; Luke 3:21; 5:16; 6:12; 9:28; 11:1. What example did Jesus give us according to these verses?

- How can we apply this to our lives?

ADDITIONAL DISCUSSION/ACTION STEPS

1. Share with group members the experiences you have had in memorizing Scripture to help you along your spiritual journey. Invite other members to share if they memorize Scripture and how it has impacted their relationship with the Lord.

2. Invite members to share methods that they use to memorize Scripture. Use one of those methods to help members memorize Romans 12:1-2. Provide 3" x 5" index cards and pens or pencils.

3. Challenge group members to choose one action they will take this week to spend more time with the Lord. Invite them to pair up with an accountability partner from the group for the remainder of this study. Encourage them to contact one another during the week to keep tabs on how they are doing in the action they have chosen to take.

TWO

THE MERCY AND FAITHFULNESS OF GOD

Objective

To help group members understand the quality of God's mercy and how to extend that mercy to others. Also to help members understand that we have a trustworthy God and how to respond in faithfulness to Him and others.

Preparation

EXERCISE 1
Prepare to read Lamentations 3:19-25. Study the background of this book.

EXERCISE 2
Invite someone—preferably one of the group members—who could lead the group in singing "Great Is Thy Faithfulness." Or obtain a copy of the song on a CD and a CD player. This will be used at the end of the session.

DISCUSSION
Familiarize yourself with the questions in the following "Group Participation" section and in the lesson, and choose which questions you definitely want to discuss with the group. Note that if you choose to do exercise 2 above, you will want to leave about 10 to 15 minutes at the end of the session for a time of praise and worship, so choose just the number of questions that you think your group will be able to discuss during the meeting time. Also prepare slips of paper with the following verses written on them: Exodus 20:6; 2 Chronicles 6:14; Psalm 32:10; Psalm 86:5; Psalm 103:11; Proverbs 28:13; Titus 3:5; Hebrews 4:16. Obtain a whiteboard, chalkboard or flipchart and felt-tip pens or chalk.

Group Participation

EXERCISE I

Give some background on the book of Lamentations. Tradition says that it was written by Jeremiah as a lament for the destruction of Jerusalem in 586 B.C. by the Babylonians after a long siege. The residents who survived were dragged off to Babylon as slaves, and the Temple was destroyed and the sacred implements looted. Yet in the midst of this lament, we find hope in these verses. Read Lamentations 3:19-25. Which verses in this passage sound familiar? What is the hope found in these verses? How does this passage speak of both the mercy and the faithfulness of God? Relate the verse to the topic of the session.

DISCUSSION

1. Discuss the following questions (or the ones you have chosen) from Part One of this week's study:

   - Read Nehemiah 9:16-31. How did the Israelites respond to God's leading? In what ways did God show His mercy to the Israelites?

   - What do Matthew 5:7 and Luke 6:36 tell us about what our response should be to God's mercy? What does it mean to be compassionate?

   - What does Zechariah 7:9-14 teach us about showing mercy and compassion? What is the promise found in Proverbs 19:17?

   - According to Deuteronomy 14:28-29; 24:19, to whom are we to show mercy, and what will the merciful receive in return? How have you experienced this in your own life? Why is it so important to God that we show mercy?

   - Read the parable of the Good Samaritan. Ask the group who the three passersby might represent (e.g., the priest might represent a religious leader; the Levite a religious layman; and the Samaritan an outcast from society). Ask how they see this occurring in today's world.

   - What was Jesus' command to the lawyer in verse 37? How can we live out this command?

2. Discuss the following questions (or the ones you have chosen) from Part Two of this week's study:

    · What do Deuteronomy 7:9; 1 Kings 8:56; Psalm 119:89-90 and Hebrews 10:23 say about how God shows His faithfulness?

    · What do 1 Peter 4:19; 1 Corinthians 10:13; Psalm 119:75 and Hebrews 12:6,10 say about our suffering in relation to God's faithfulness?

    · What is the astounding statement about God's faithfulness found in 2 Timothy 2:13? What does this tell you about the nature of God?

    · What other things is God faithfully doing for us according to 1 Corinthians 1:8-9; 1 Thessalonians 5:23-24 and 2 Thessalonians 3:3?

    · Read Galatians 5:22-23. What does this verse say about our faithfulness? What are some ways we can show faithfulness according to the verses listed in this section?

    · What are some of the results and/or rewards of being faithful?

ADDITIONAL DISCUSSION/ACTION STEPS
1. Hand out the slips of paper with the Scripture references on them to volunteers. Ask them to read their assigned verse and state what the verse tells us about God's mercy and to whom He extends it. Summarize their responses on the board or chart. Invite volunteers to share which verse is most meaningful to them.

2. Read Lamentations 3:22-23. Encourage members to memorize this verse.

3. Discuss some practical ways that we can share God's mercy with others. What are some practical ways that we can show our faithfulness to God? To others?

4. Invite volunteers to briefly share ways in which they have experienced God's mercy and/or faithfulness.

EXERCISE 2

Reread Lamentations 3:22-23 and lead the group in singing "Great Is Thy Faithfulness." Close with prayer to encourage members to be faithful in their commitments to the Lord and to show mercy to others.

THREE

THE GOODNESS OF GOD

Objective

To help group members understand the many expressions of God's goodness and how they can show His goodness to others.

Preparation

EXERCISE 1

During the week, call group members and ask them to ask three to five people how they would define goodness. Ask them to bring the responses to the meeting. Obtain a whiteboard, chalkboard or flipchart and felt-tip pens or chalk.

EXERCISE 2

Prepare for a reading of Psalm 136. You will read the beginning of each verse and the group members will repeat the chorus "His love endures forever." This will be done as a concluding activity.

DISCUSSION

Familiarize yourself with the questions in the following "Group Participation" section, and choose which questions you definitely want to discuss with the group.

Group Participation

EXERCISE 1

Invite several volunteers to share the responses they received when they asked their three to five people about how they would define goodness. As they share, summarize the responses on the board or chart. Invite members to list some of the things they know about God's goodness. Discuss the differences between the worldly concept of goodness and God's goodness.

DISCUSSION

1. Discuss the following questions (or the ones you have chosen) from the "A Closer Look at God's Truth" section:

    •   What material blessings does God give us out of His goodness as recorded in Matthew 5:45 and Acts 14:17? Invite group members to share one material blessing the Lord has given them in His goodness.

    •   What were the spiritual blessings given to the Israelites by the Lord as recorded in Isaiah 63:7-9?

    •   What are the good things that God has stored up for those who fear Him according to Psalm 31:19-24? Invite group members to share the spiritual blessings they have received from God. Read 1 Corinthians 2:9 aloud and invite members to respond to what this verse says to them.

    •   What do Psalm 107:9 and Luke 1:53 say about the main prerequisite to being satisfied with God's goodness?

    •   What are the conditions for true satisfaction found in Psalm 81:8-16? What results does He promise us in these verses?

    •   According to Isaiah 55:1-2, what is our spiritual condition apart from God and what is the result when we partake of what God offers?

    •   Read Psalm 103:1-5 aloud. What is the promise in these verses?

    •   What do 2 Corinthians 9:8; Galatians 6:9-10 and Hebrews 13:16 say about showing God's goodness to others?

2. Discuss the following questions (or the ones you have chosen) from the "A Closer Look at My Own Heart" section:

- How should understanding that God in His goodness is storing up good things for us and that He has a perfect plan for us change our attitudes and lifestyles?

- How does realizing God's goodness toward us affect our attitudes during difficult times?

ADDITIONAL DISCUSSION/ACTION STEPS
1. Discuss how we respond to God's goodness and some of the practical ways that we can show God's goodness to others.

2. Ask participants to explain what are the most meaningful aspects of God's goodness to them. How can their personal expression of that particular aspect make them more like Jesus?

4. Encourage group members to continue to memorize meaningful Scripture verses from each week's lesson.

EXERCISE 2
For a concluding exercise, do a choral reading of Psalm 136 with you reading the beginning of each verse and the group responding with "His love endures forever." Invite group members to add their own statement about God's goodness and have the group respond with "His love endures forever."

FOUR

𝒯HE WISDOM OF GOD

Objective

To help group members understand that God's wisdom is trustworthy and that His wisdom is available to them for the asking.

Preparation

EXERCISE 1

Collect examples of worldly wisdom that are in opposition to God's wisdom. For example, "The world says it is all right to cheat on your income taxes [tell 'white' lies, break the speed laws, and so forth] as long as it doesn't hurt anyone or you don't get caught." You should be able to find examples from the media, but also listen to conversations you have with others. Jot down examples as you hear or see them. (As an option, call group members during the week and have them be on the lookout for examples.)

EXERCISE 2

Collect several magazines and newspapers. Obtain a poster board for every four to five group members, scissors, felt-tip pens and glue.

DISCUSSION

Familiarize yourself with the questions in the following "Group Participation" section, and choose which questions you definitely want to discuss with the group.

Group Participation

EXERCISE 1

Share some of the examples of worldly wisdom that you have collected. Invite group members to share any examples they might have. Discuss what they learned about God's wisdom that is counter to the worldly examples. Invite members to suggest any verses they learned this week (or in past weeks) that counter the worldly wisdom.

EXERCISE 2
Divide the group into smaller groups of about four to five. Give each group a few magazines, a piece of poster board, a pair of scissors, pens and glue. Instruct them to look for examples of worldly wisdom that is counter to God's wisdom, cut them out and glue them to the poster board. Have groups share their posters. Read 1 Corinthians 1:18-31 and instruct them to write verse 25 across their posters.

DISCUSSION
1. Discuss the following questions (or the ones you have chosen) from the "A Closer Look at God's Truth" section:

   • What do Job 37:14-16; Psalm 139:1-6; Psalm 147:4-5; Isaiah 40:28 and Daniel 2:20-22 say about the extent of God's wisdom?

   • What does Isaiah 55:8-9 say about the difference between God's thoughts and our thoughts? Because we cannot fully understand God's ways and thoughts, how are we to pray?

   • According to Jeremiah 10:12, how is God's wisdom manifested in His creation? How do John 3:16 and Ephesians 1:7-8 express God's ultimate wisdom for us?

   • How does Colossians 2:2-3 describe Christ? What did Paul say was the genuine knowledge that Christians have?

   • Read 1 Corinthians 1:18-31 aloud. What does verse 25 say about the world's wisdom? How have you seen evidence of this in the world today? How has God used what the world deems as foolish, weak, lowly or despised?

   • Read Psalm 111:10. How can the fear of the Lord be the beginning of wisdom?

   • According to James 1:5-6, how do we receive divine wisdom? What is the role of the Holy Spirit in attaining godly wisdom?

- According to Colossians 3:16, what is another source of God's wisdom? What does 2 Timothy 3:15-16 say are the purposes of Scripture?

2. Discuss the following questions from the "A Closer Look at My Own Heart" section:

- What conclusions can be made from Galatians 1:15-16 and 1 Peter 1:1-2 about our all-wise and all-knowing God?

- What did you learn from your self-evaluation? Invite volunteers to share some of their answers.

ADDITIONAL DISCUSSION/ACTION STEPS

1. Discuss some of the ways we can learn to understand God's wisdom.

2. Invite volunteers to share how they have experienced the Holy Spirit's help in understanding God's wisdom.

3. Continue to encourage group members to memorize Scripture and express their spiritual journey in their journaling. Invite a couple of volunteers to share how either of these activities has helped them understand the Lord's wisdom.

FIVE

THE OMNIPOTENCE OF GOD

Objective

To help group members understand that they can ask for the Lord's power to do what He asks them to do, even if it seems impossible, and that His strength is activated through our dependence on Him.

Preparation

EXERCISE 1

Is there someone in your group or church family who has experienced a true miracle from God—an example of God doing the impossible? If so, enlist this person to give a brief testimony of what God did. Ask the person to share some Scripture verses that especially spoke to him or her during this experience.

EXERCISE 2

This will be used as a concluding exercise. Obtain enough pieces of poster board and felt-tip pens to have one for every four group members. Also provide sheets of paper and pens or pencils.

DISCUSSION

Familiarize yourself with the questions in the following "Group Participation" section, and choose which questions you definitely want to discuss with the group. Note that if you choose to do exercise 2 above, you will want to leave about 8 to 10 minutes at the end of the session, so choose just the number of questions that you think your group will be able to discuss during the meeting time.

Group Participation

EXERCISE I

Invite the person you have enlisted to share his or her brief testimony of God's omnipotence. Ask him or her to share the Scriptures that were especially helpful during this time. Allow a few minutes for group members to ask questions.

DISCUSSION

1. Discuss the following questions (or the ones you have chosen) from the "A Closer Look at God's Truth" section:

   • What words or phrases are used to describe God's power in Genesis 35:11; Job 42:2; Psalm 91:1; John 1:49 and Revelation 11:17? What does Jesus say about God's omnipotence in Matthew 19:26? How can these descriptions of God's power encourage you in difficult times?

   • Read Psalm 33:6-9 aloud. If God is in control of nature, why are there earthquakes, tornadoes and floods? How might these natural disasters be used for God's purposes?

   • What does Daniel 2:20-21; 4:24-25 say about God's power in human government? What are some other ways God controls nations?

   • According to Hebrews 1:14, what is the function of angels? How could that knowledge be a comfort to us?

   • How does Job 1:12; 2:3-6 illustrate God's power over Satan? How might that be an encouragement to us?

   • How is God's power over sickness demonstrated in Matthew 8:14-17? How is His power over demons shown in Mark 1:23-28? How did Jesus demonstrate God's power over death in John 10:17-18; 11:43-44?

   • According to Luke 1:25-55, what was impossible about this event in human terms? What was Mary's response?

- How did Asa demonstrate his obedience to God in 2 Chronicles 14? In what seemingly hopeless situation was Asa and the nation of Judah? How did Asa respond? What was the result?

- Read 2 Corinthians 12:9-10 aloud. How have you seen this to be true? In what ways should this change our attitudes toward our own weaknesses and the weaknesses of others?

2. Discuss the following questions (or the ones you have chosen) from the "A Closer Look at My Own Heart" section:

- How can the fact of God's omnipotence encourage us in our own difficult circumstances?

- How can our deepened understanding of our omnipotent God transform us more into the likeness of Jesus Christ?

ADDITIONAL DISCUSSION/ACTION STEPS

1. Invite group members to share how they have experienced the omnipotence of God in their own lives.

2. Unbelievers often challenge Christians with the question, "If God is all-powerful and loving, why does He allow natural disasters, accidents, illness [and so forth] to happen?" How would you answer this question?

EXERCISE 2

As a conclusion to this session, challenge the group members to write psalms that praise God's omnipotence. Psalm 33:6-9 could be used as a model. Divide the group into smaller groups of three to four people and give each group some paper, pens or pencils, a piece of poster board and a felt-tip pen. Instruct them to write a psalm about God's omnipotence. They can use the paper to jot down ideas as they work on this. Allow about 8 to 10 minutes for this exercise, and then have each group share its psalm.

SIX

THE HOLINESS OF GOD

Objective

To help group members understand that even though holiness seems lofty and impossible for us to attain, we can be holy as He is holy through the power of Jesus' blood and His Holy Spirit.

Preparation

EXERCISE I
Write the following Scripture references on separate slips of paper: Exodus 15:11; Isaiah 5:16; Isaiah 40:25; Hosea 11:9 and Revelation 4:8.

EXERCISE 2
Prepare a dramatic reading of Isaiah 6:1-5 and Revelation 4. Obtain a CD of instrumental worship music and a CD player (or use a laptop computer or MP3 player). (As an option, have someone in your group who can play the piano or guitar play during the reading.) Select a few worship songs to sing after this exercise or for a concluding time of worship—an ideal song would be "I See the Lord" by Chris Falson. (For another option, obtain several candles, candleholders and a lighter, and safely place these around the room.)

DISCUSSION
Familiarize yourself with the questions in the following "Group Participation" section, and choose which questions you definitely want to discuss with the group.

Group Participation

EXERCISE I
Invite volunteers to read Exodus 15:11; Isaiah 5:16; Isaiah 40:25; Hosea 11:9 and Revelation 4:8. Discuss what each of these descriptions tells us

about God's holiness. What does it mean to be holy? When we say God is holy, what does that really mean?

EXERCISE 2

Instruct group members to close their eyes. If possible, lower the lights in the room and have several candles lit. Ask the group to draw a picture in their minds as you read. Start the instrumental worship music CD and read Isaiah 6:1-5 and Revelation 4 aloud. Allow the room to remain totally quiet for a minute or two, allowing members to complete the pictures in their minds. (Note that this could also be a concluding exercise for this session.) Finish the exercise by singing a worship song or two.

DISCUSSION

1. Discuss the following questions (or the ones you have chosen) from the "A Closer Look at God's Truth" section:

    *   What can be concluded about God's holiness in the follow-ing Scripture passages: Genesis 6:5-7; Psalm 5:4-6; Proverbs 15:9; John 3:16? How did God demonstrate His holiness to humankind?

    *   What does Isaiah 57:15 tell us about God's desire for His people? How were the Israelites described by God in Exodus 19:6 and Deuteronomy 7:6?

    *   What does God command of His people in Leviticus 18:3-4; 19:2? According to 1 Peter 1:15-16, what is God's will for us?

    *   What are the five names given to believers in 1 Peter 2:9-10? How do those names compare to what God called the Israelites in Exodus 19:6 and Deuteronomy 7:6?

    *   What does it mean to you that God chose you before the creation of the world to be holy and blameless in His sight (see Ephesians 1:4)? How do we become holy according to Colossians 1:13 and 1 John 1:9?

    *   Read Isaiah 6:1-8. What did Isaiah exclaim when he found himself in the presence of Holy God? What did the Lord do for him to make him fit for service? How must we prepare for serving the Lord in holiness?

- According to 2 Peter 1:3-4, what has God provided for us to share in His divine nature?

- What part does discipline play in making us holy according to Hebrews 12:10-11? How have you experienced this truth?

2. Discuss the following question (or the ones you have chosen) from the "A Closer Look at My Own Heart" section:

- What steps must be taken to become more holy?

- How can you commit to following these steps to holiness?

ADDITIONAL DISCUSSION/ACTION STEPS
1. Discuss how you would explain the holiness of God to an unbeliever. How can we live holy lives in an unholy world?

2. If you have already done Exercise 2, have the group spend a time in prayer and confession, committing to the steps that were discussed in the "A Closer Look at My Own Heart" section. Close with a worship song.

SEVEN

THE GRACE OF GOD

Objective

To help group members understand the marvelous grace that God has extended to us and how to extend that same grace to others.

Preparation

EXERCISE

Purchase a nice gift that anyone in the group might enjoy. It could even be a gift card to a restaurant, coffee shop or a store. Wrap it up in a beautifully prepared box. Obtain a timer or a watch with an alarm.

DISCUSSION

Familiarize yourself with the questions in the following "Group Participation" section, and choose which questions you definitely want to discuss with the group.

Group Participation

EXERCISE

At the beginning of the meeting when everyone is seated, set the timer for 30 seconds and hand the gift-wrapped box to the person nearest to you. Tell the members to keep passing the box until the time is up. The person holding the box gets to keep the gift. Have her unwrap the gift. Relate the unexpected gift to how God's grace is given. Invite group members to give a definition of God's grace.

DISCUSSION

1. Discuss the following questions (or the ones you have chosen) from the "A Closer Look at God's Truth" section:

- How is God's graciousness described in Exodus 34:6 and Nehemiah 9:17? How is Jesus' graciousness described in Psalm 45:2; Luke 2:40 and Luke 4:22?

- How is God's grace described in Romans 5:17; 2 Corinthians 12:9 and Ephesians 1:6-7? What is your understanding of God's grace? What is your personal experience with God's grace?

- According to Ephesians 2:1-3, what was our spiritual condition before His grace was exercised in our lives? What are the results of God's grace in our lives as recorded in Titus 2:11 and Titus 3:5-7?

- Invite members to read their paraphrase of Ephesians 2:8-9. What is the one ingredient we must have to appropriate God's grace for our salvation? Although God freely offers salvation to every person, why do only some receive it?

- According to 2 Corinthians 8:9; 2 Corinthians 12:9; Galatians 1:15; 2 Thessalonians 2:16; 2 Timothy 2:1; Hebrews 4:16 and Hebrews 13:9, what are the other benefits besides salvation that God has given us by His grace?

- What does Ephesians 2:10 tell us that we are created to do? How does that relate to the grace we have been given as described in verses 8-9?

- How do Ephesians 4:29,32 and 1 Peter 4:10 instruct us to minister the grace of God to others? According to 2 Corinthians 8:7 and 9:6-8, what are other ways we can minister grace?

2. Discuss the following questions from the "A Closer Look at My Own Heart" section:

- Remembering the grace God has given us, what should be our attitude toward others? How can we show His grace to others every day?

- How can we make sure that the good deeds we do glorify God and not ourselves?

- What bad attitudes or actions might we need to watch for when serving others in order that God's grace is preeminent?

ADDITIONAL DISCUSSION/ACTION STEPS

1. Discuss how the truth that our salvation is the gift of our gracious God should affect us. How should knowing that there is nothing we can do to earn His salvation affect us?

2. Discuss some practical ways the group members can show God's grace to others.

3. Read Romans 12:6-8; 1 Corinthians 12:28 and 1 Peter 4:9-11. Discuss how these spiritual gifts can be used to minister God's grace to others. Challenge members to investigate their spiritual gifts and to use them to help others.

$\mathcal{T}$HE LOVE OF GOD

Objective

To help group members understand the varied aspects of God's love and how they can express that love to those around them.

Preparation

EXERCISE 1

On a whiteboard, chalkboard or flipchart, draw a chart with the following phrases written across the top: "God's Love Is . . ." and "Even When . . ." Draw a line down the middle between the two phrases.

EXERCISE 2

Collect examples of the world's definition of love throughout the week. Your sources might be newspapers, magazines, TV shows or even comments that people make. (As an option, you could also call group members during the week and ask them to ask five people, "How do you define love?" Encourage them to ask people who do not have a Christian worldview.)

EXERCISE 3

Obtain a worship CD and a CD player, or invite someone—preferably one of the group members—to lead the group in singing two or three praise and worship songs. The songs will be used at the end of the session. Choose two or three worship songs that tell of God's love.

DISCUSSION

Familiarize yourself with the questions in the following "Group Participation" section, and choose which questions you definitely want to discuss with the group. Note that if you choose to do exercise 3 above, you will want to leave about 10 to 15 minutes at the end of the session for a time of praise and worship, so choose just the number of questions that you think your group will be able to discuss during the meeting time.

Group Participation

EXERCISE 1

Invite a volunteer to read 1 Corinthians 13. Ask group members to call out the qualities of God's love that are listed in this Scripture passage. As they do, write their responses under the "God's Love Is . . ." column. After you have listed all (or most) of the qualities, ask members to respond to the second column with a suggestion of things that try our *agape* love. For example, for the word "patient," someone might suggest "even when a child is moving slowly on a busy day." Or, for the phrase "does not envy," the suggestion might be "even when my neighbor gets a brand-new car." Discuss why it is hard to always show Christlike love to people. What can we do to remind ourselves to love others with the same love God shows to us? How can we love someone who is difficult to love?

EXERCISE 2

Share the samples of the worldly understanding of love that you have collected. Invite group members to share any examples they have observed. If you did the optional preparation, ask members to share the answers they received from the question they asked people about how they would define love. Relate these views to God's love that was discussed in this week's lesson.

DISCUSSION

1. Discuss the following questions (or the ones you have chosen) from the "A Closer Look at God's Truth" section:

   • How does 1 John 4:8,16 characterize God? How is His love described in Jeremiah 31:3; Romans 5:8; Ephesians 2:4 and Ephesians 3:18?

   • According to Matthew 3:17; John 3:16; John 14:21; John 16:27 and Romans 5:8, who are the recipients of God's love? Where do you fall into this list? Who does Jesus love? How did He demonstrate His love?

   • What are some of the ways the Father has shown His love to us? Invite volunteers to share how they have experienced any of these manifestations of God's love.

- How did God demonstrate the sacrificial aspect of His love? We have seen that God has the attribute of love and how He demonstrates it to us. How then do we respond to His love? How can we love the way He loves?

- What do Romans 5:5; 1 Timothy 1:14 and 2 Timothy 1:7 say about how and why we can love others as God loves us?

- According to Matthew 5:44; John 15:12; Ephesians 1:15; Ephesians 5:25; 1 Thessalonians 3:12 and Titus 2:4, whom are we commanded to love? List the answers on the board or chart.

- Why is *agape* love the greatest gift of all?

2. Discuss the following questions (or the ones you have chosen) from the "A Closer Look at My Own Heart" section:

- What do Galatians 5:13; Galatians 6:2,10; Ephesians 4:32; Philippians 2:4 and 1 John 3:17-18 say about ministering in love?

- What are practical ways that we can demonstrate our love for God?

ADDITIONAL DISCUSSION/ACTION STEPS

1. Discuss practical ways that we can demonstrate God's love to each of the different kinds of people we are to love. As an option, divide the group into seven smaller groups. Assign each group one of the different types of people (e.g., neighbors, enemies, one another in the group, fellow believers, our spouses, our children) whom we are commanded to love. Ask them to suggest ways that they can show love using the list of the different types of love. After a few minutes, ask the small groups to share their ideas.

2. Discuss why it is often harder to show unconditional love to our family members or to fellow believers than it is to show love to complete strangers or mere acquaintances.

3. Discuss what is the ultimate act of sharing God's love with others. (The answer is leading others to Jesus and to salvation.) How can showing

God's love to others lead them to want to know more about God and accept His gift of salvation?

EXERCISE 3
Conclude this Bible study with a time of praise and worship, thanking the Lord for all He has done for the group members. Invite the group members to share a lesson they have learned about God's character from this study during the past eight weeks. Pray Philippians 1:9-11 in unison from the end of chapter 8, and then conclude by singing two or three praise and worship songs.

What Is Aglow International?

From one nation to 172 worldwide...
From one fellowship to more than 4,600...
From 100 people to more than 17 million...

Aglow International has experienced phenomenal growth since its inception 40 years ago. In 1967, four women from the state of Washington prayed for a way to reach out to other Christian women in simple fellowship, free from denominational boundaries.

The first meeting held in Seattle, Washington, USA, drew more than 100 women to a local hotel. From that modest beginning, Aglow International has become one of the largest intercultural, interdenominational women's organizations in the world.

Each year, an estimated 17 million people are ministered to through Aglow's local fellowship meetings, Bible studies, support groups, retreats, conferences and various outreaches. From the inner city to the upper echelons, from the woman next door to the corporate executive, Aglow seeks to minister to the felt needs of women around the world.

Christian women find Aglow a "safe place" to grow spiritually and begin to discover and use the gifts, talents and abilities God has given them. Aglow offers excellent leadership training and varied opportunities to develop those leadership skills.

Undergirding the evangelistic thrust of the ministry is an emphasis on prayer, which has led to an active prayer network linking six continents. The vast prayer power available through Aglow women around the world is being used by God to influence countless lives in families, communities, cities and nations.

Aglow's Mission Statement

Our mission is to lead women to Jesus Christ and provide opportunity for Christian women to grow in their faith and minister to others.

—⟆∿⟅—

Aglow's Continuing Focus...

- To reconcile a woman to her womanhood as God designed. To strengthen and empower her to fulfill the unfolding plan of God as He brings restoration to the male/female relationship, which is the foundation of the home, the church and the community.
- To love women of all cultures, with a special focus on Muslim women.
- To reach out to every strata of society, from inner cities to isolated outposts to our own neighborhoods, with very practical and tangible expressions of the love of Jesus.

—⟆∿⟅—

Aglow Ministers In...

Albania, Angola, Anguilla, Antigua, Argentina, Aruba, Australia, Austria, Bahamas, Bahrain, Barbados, Belarus, Belgium, Belize, Benin, Bermuda, Bolivia, Botswana, Brazil, Britain, Bulgaria, Burkina Faso, Cameroon, Canada, Chile, China, Colombia, Congo (Dem. Rep. of), Congo (Rep. of), Costa Rica, Côte d'Ivoire, Cuba, Curaçao, Czech Republic, Denmark, Djibouti, Dominica, Dominican Republic, Ecuador, Egypt, El Salvador, Equatorial Guinea, Estonia, Ethiopia, Faroe Islands, Fiji, Finland, France, Gabon, the Gambia, Germany, Ghana, Grand Cayman, Greece, Grenada, Guam, Guatemala, Guinea, Guyana, Haiti, Honduras, Hungary, Iceland, India, Indonesia, Ireland, Israel, Jamaica, Japan, Kazakstan, Kenya, Korea, Kyrgyzstan, Latvia, Lithuania, Malawi, Malaysia, Mali, Mauritius, Mexico, Mongolia, Mozambique, Myanmar, Nepal, Netherlands, New Zealand, Nicaragua, Niger, Nigeria, Norway, Oman, Pakistan, Panama, Papua New Guinea, Peru, Philippines, Portugal, Puerto Rico, Romania, Russia, Rwanda, Samoa, Samoa (American), Scotland, Senegal, Serbia, Sierra Leone, Singapore, South Africa, Spain, Sri Lanka, St. Kitts, St. Lucia, St. Maartan, St. Vincent, Sudan, Suriname, Sweden, Switzerland, Tajikistan, Tanzania, Thailand, Togo, Tonga, Trinidad/Tobago, Turks & Caicos Islands, Uganda, Ukraine, United States, Uruguay, Uzbekistan, Venezuela, Vietnam, Virgin Islands (American), Virgin Islands (British), Wales, Yugoslavia, Zambia, Zimbabwe, and other nations.

How do I find my nearest Aglow Fellowship? Call or write us at:

AGLOW.
INTITLED: INTERNATIONAL

P.O. Box 1749, Edmonds, WA 98020-1749
Phone: 425-775-7282 or 1-800-793-8126
Fax: 425-778-9615   E-mail: aglow@aglow.org
Web site: http://www.aglow.org/

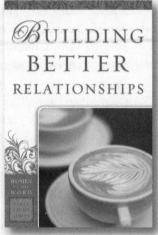
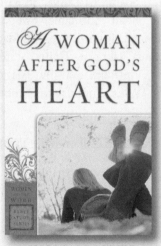
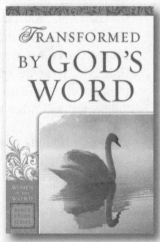